Live in Vibrant Health

Live in Vibrant Health

A God-upgraded Vision
of Health that Shines
from the Inside Out

Stephanie Tyler, ND

download book resources at
LiveinVibrantHealth.com

Copyright ©2023 by Stephanie Tyler, All Rights Reserved.
LiveInVibrantHealth.com

No portion of this book may be reproduced in any form without written permission from the author, except as permitted by U.S. copyright law.

Scripture quotations marked NASB are taken from the New American Standard Bible®, Copyright ©1960, 1971, 1977, 1995 by the Lockman Foundation. Used by permission. Lockman.org

Scripture quotations marked ESV are from The ESV® Bible (The Holy Bible, English Standard Version®), copyright © 2001 by Crossway, a publishing ministry of Good News Publishers. Used by permission. All rights reserved.

Scripture quotations marked TPT are from The Passion Translation®. Copyright © 2017, 2018, 2020 by Passion & Fire Ministries, Inc. Used by permission. All rights reserved. ThePassionTranslation.com.

Scripture quotations marked NIV are taken from the Holy Bible, New International Version®, NIV®. Copyright © 1973, 1978, 1984, 2011 by Biblica, Inc.™ Used by permission of Zondervan. All rights reserved worldwide. www.zondervan.com.

Scripture quotations marked NKJV are taken from the New King James Version®. Copyright © 1982 by Thomas Nelson. Used by permission. All rights reserved.

Scripture quotations marked KJV are taken from the Holy Bible, King James Version.

Scripture quotations marked NLT are taken from the Holy Bible, New Living Translation, Copyright © 1996, 2004, 2015 by Tyndale House Foundation. Used by permission of Tyndale House Publishers, Inc., Carol Stream, Illinois 60188. All rights reserved.

Scripture quotations marked MSG are taken from The Message, copyright © 1993, 2002, 2018 by Eugene H. Peterson. Used by permission of NavPress. All rights reserved. Represented by Tyndale House Publishers.

for my children, grandchildren and future generations

*We will not hide these truths from our children;
we will tell the next generation about the glorious deeds
of the Lord, about his power and his mighty wonders.
Psalm 78:4 NLT*

Contents

9	Introduction: Will You Join Me?
13	How to Use This Book
15	Mission One - Say Yes
21	Mission Two - Discover a Higher Purpose for Healthy
31	Mission Three - Work Inside Out
43	Mission Four - Embrace the Process for Transformation
53	Mission Five - Connect with the Heart of God
69	Mission Six - Come into Agreement with the Father
81	Mission Seven - Experience Freedom
93	Mission Eight - Fit and Fueled to Run with Purpose
107	Mission Nine - Live to Shine
115	Vibrant Health Framework™

Why Jesus?
Write the Word - Who God Says I Am
References
About the Author

INTRODUCTION

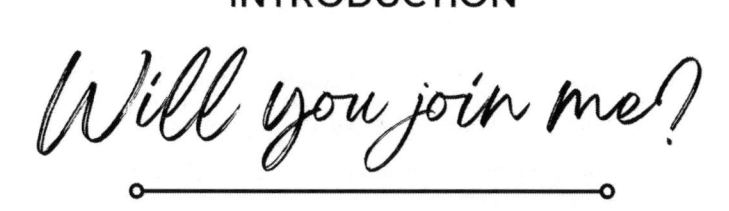

Will you join me?

The Serenity Prayer:
   God grant me the serenity
   To accept the things I cannot change;
   Courage to change the things I can;
   And wisdom to know the difference.

Ladies (and especially us mamas) don't really accept things we "cannot change" because we think we can fix it all!

Am I right?!

As mothers, we wear many hats and are the "glue" that holds the family together. But this position as "master fixer" gives us a false sense of control. I have been a master fixer for quite some time! What about you?

But eventually, something causes too big a strain and you can't keep it all under control! Some can hold on and 'white-knuckle' through longer than others, but eventually there's a point where you get stretched too thin and you find your breaking point.

Have you been there? Are you there now?
Do you keep pushing and striving?
Is it taking its toll on your health, energy, and mood? Or straining your relationships?

I see you! I am you! And I'm here to say that God has a better way!

I believe God walked me through and gave me breakthrough! I'm still a work in progress, but I am more confident as His daughter and walking in more freedom than I've ever experienced before. I am confident He's called me to walk in vibrant health and shine for Him AND to call you to do it too! That's what I want for you—confidence in who you are in Christ and in His purpose for you, a shining light in this crazy world.

How did God call me to walk in vibrant health and live to shine?

I could tell you about the loss of a child, about a business that failed or walking away from a huge project I loved. But there were two big course corrections where God really changed my journey, especially when it comes to living in joy and on purpose for Him.

The first course correction started with my father's cancer diagnosis around his 50th birthday. Fear drove my father and me to do a lot of research. As he read more about the side effects of conventional treatment, the more he sought out other options. The negative side of the Internet and so much available information is being overwhelmed! We were surely overwhelmed!

Through the four years of battling cancer, my dad was alive, but he wasn't living. If you've seen a cancer patient go through treatment, you know what I'm talking about. They are just not able to live a vibrant life. They cannot be a supportive spouse, a great employee, a loving father, or grandfather. They often can't attend church, family gatherings, or serve others. The list of things they can't do is long.

Through fear and overwhelm my dad made hard choices that involved some natural protocols and some conventional. In the end, he lost his earthly battle and entered heaven at the age of 54.

After his diagnosis and the research, I decided I needed a framework from which to process all that I was learning. I enrolled in Trinity School of Natural Health and devoted my time to learning all I could—this was definitely a change of purpose in life.

Through my new expertise as a Naturopath, I wanted to "cancer-proof" my life and the life of the rest of my family. I didn't want history to be repeated. I couldn't "fix" my father, but I was hopeful I could "fix" the rest of my family. In the years since, I have amassed quite a library including many journals full of notes on all things natural health. I have studied Gerson, Budwig, Henderson, Rife and others who have made names for themselves in natural cancer protocols. I've studied different diets, supplements, and herbs. I've collected tools such as a juicer, whole body vibration machine, BioMat, and a frequency generator to name a few. There was a time that I truly believed that there was a perfect diet to heal every physical disease. But now, several years later, I believe I've learned that all these physical things aren't the full picture or even the most significant piece of the puzzle.

Struggles in my own life and those around me revealed that focusing on a perfect diet and the perfect supplements will leave a person striving and empty. I started my wellness coaching practice seeing clients who didn't need diet advice or any miracle pills; they needed Jesus. They needed inner healing of past hurts that only Jesus can accomplish. They needed to kindle (or rekindle) their relationship with Jesus. In these spiritual matters, I felt unequipped to help them (I couldn't fix them either!) While I didn't have the expertise to help them, I knew that attending to their spirit and soul was the missing piece of the puzzle.

I continued to study different modalities, protocols, and others' work in the natural health field, always looking for pieces to the "cancer-proof your life" puzzle. Big storm number two, however, was brewing in my home. Enter course correction number two: trying to control and hide my husband's alcohol addiction. As a "master fixer" I felt helpless and at a loss as to what to do.

I had been treading water, barely keeping my head up. But the day came when I felt the water rushing over my head and it was there, I found my breaking point. I felt a panic attack coming on. I fled my house and found a quiet spot to sit with the Lord, where I poured out my heart and my pain. I fully surrendered all my expectations and dreams to the Lord that day. One of the hardest days of my life became a life-changing course correction.

All my stress and striving were coming from a place of fear. Fear of losing people I loved, first my dad and then my husband. Fear made me feel anxious, stressed, and desperate to regain control. While the issues and the solutions had been brewing for a while, God really started a new work in me through Revelation Wellness instructor training and then Holy Yoga training. It's crazy that moving the body influences one's soul and spirit, but it did. I had no idea what I was signing up for and why I was so drawn to it. However, that's when God began really showing me how important the spiritual aspect was for true health.

We'll look at it all more in depth, but what I'm sharing with you here is an inside-out approach to health that keeps Jesus at the center. One that flows from spirit and soul out to your physical body. It's what I believe is missing in the health and wellness industry!

Today as I write this, it is in full praise of the work that God alone has done (in me and my husband). Through these two big course corrections He solidified my identity, restored joy and peace and gave me purpose!

God brought breakthrough from letting fear control my life and gave me victory in living to shine! I'm still working out all the truth He's shown me. I'm not the perfect example, but I am walking now with a measure of success! I want that same breakthrough for you—not just physical health but a whole body transformation so you feel vibrant and joyful from the inside out and free to live on purpose for Jesus in a lost world regardless of your circumstances. So, I'm asking if you'll give me permission to guide you through all God has shown me?

Will you make a choice to leave behind the stress and striving?
I don't want to see you stuck and struggling any longer!

Will you join me?
Let's get started!

Stephanie

How to use this book

This book is the cleaned-up version of the journey God had for me. As you read, know that the missions are in a purposeful order, so I think it's best to not skip around. Stay on each mission as long as you need before moving on to the next one. You may find repeating the missions helpful as God leads. There is always opportunity for growth, and I know I'll cycle back through the missions as well.

For any male readers, the principles apply to you too! But as a woman, I decided that I needed to just tell my story to the women that I saw struggling with some of the same things that I was struggling with.

Things You'll Encounter on this Journey

Do not merely listen to the word, and so deceive yourselves. Do what it says. James 1:22 NIV

"Go Forward"
When you come to a "Go Forward" stop reading and put into action different activities to solidify the principles in this book.

"Interact with the Word"
There are places to journal in this book but you may want a notebook to journal as well. You are encouraged to record the prayers and whatever you learn from the Lord during your time together.

"Pile up your memorial stones"
Often an author will give summary points at the end of a chapter to highlight or call your attention to the main points, but not me. This is all about YOUR journey. I want you to record your summary and the truths God showed you that you feel is important to YOUR journey.

"Obstacle" or "Sabotage"
This may or may not apply to you, but please prayerfully consider whether there is a need to remove it to continue on your journey.

"Roadblock"
A roadblock is more of a stronghold that completely blocks the way. We need to stop and examine any lies we might be believing. We will need to replace the lies with God's truths so we can renew our mind and continue our journey.

Why did you bring Jesus into this?
What if you don't know Jesus? What if he's not really your jam—or maybe you just need a little more info to understand why this book involves Jesus.
If so, then I invite you to start this book—at the end of the book! The Appendix will tell you "WHY JESUS" and how you can know who He is and how He could be the missing piece to your life!

Finally, I'd like to give a bit of a warning. You will likely face some difficulties through this journey; press in and don't give up. This book is thin and the steps are simple. But simple isn't always easy. You will be diving into a lot of God's Word and there's lots more we could unpack! I recommend that you grab a friend to go through the book with so you can hold each other accountable and help each other go deeper if its needed.

If you need a community and coaching to go with this book to see the transformation you are after then I strongly suggest you join me in the "Vibrant Woman Reignited" program. VibrantWomanReignited.com

MISSION ONE

Say Yes

Your days will be most joyful, your heart will be most free and your mind will be most at peace when you've said Yes to Him." - Jess Connolly [1]

"At the end of the introduction, I asked if you'd go with me on this journey. I hope you gave a big YES!

But you might be asking, yes to what?
Say yes to taking the journey through the missions in this book and letting God transform you!

Then I heard the voice of the LORD saying, "Whom shall I send, and who will go for Us?" Then I said, "Here am I, send me!" Isaiah 6:8 NIV

Say, "YES, God, I'm ready to travel with You! I'm ready for more!"
Tell the Lord now, "Here am I, send me."

Explain to me, Where exactly?
We are going on a journey that transforms you into a healthy vibrant woman. A woman full of peace and joy that lives life on purpose. This journey will take you through throwing off the old fleshly ways and blossoming into the new creation God made you to be.

Does that sound like a journey you want to travel?
If you are tired of living in fear and anxiety.... let's go!
If you are done being weary, bitter, and stuck...let's go!
If you are ready to quit striving...let's go!

In the above verse Isaiah says, "Send me" and that implies action. We live in a time when we are overloaded with information. Information alone will not bring you transformation. It's time to put some feet on your faith.

In these missions you'll read part of my stories and the things I learned and how I learned them. Then I'll ask you to go deeper to keep walking and growing—to activate God's truths and let them transform you.

The LORD said to Moses, "Why do you cry to me? Tell the people of Israel to go forward." Exodus 14:15 ESV

I'm going to tell you the same thing, "Go Forward." Please do not read this book for knowledge. Use it as a tool to go on mission with God. As you read, you'll encounter sections that call you to "go forward." That means to stop reading and act before you read any further.

Go Forward: Begin Your Journaling Practice
Journaling is the first action I'm asking you to put into practice. Journaling, I've found, is something people either love or hate. It forces a person to stop and be still, talk to God, assess emotions and so much more. As a busy, stressed, and striving mom, it definitely was not something I wanted to do. I just wanted to push on. But now, looking back, it's one of the best things I ever did. If this is really out of your comfort zone, don't worry, I'll be guiding you through as we go.

Start now - Write out a prayer to the Lord giving Him your YES to go on this journey with Him. It doesn't have to be long; it can be as short as Isaiah - "Here am I, send me" but do take the time to write it out. (There is some brain science to writing it out and not just saying it quickly in your mind—just trust me and write it out.) After you write it out, say it out loud to the Lord as well.

If the need for perfectionism keeps you from being honest with yourself and writing in this book—then grab a cheap notebook so you can be messy!

Go Forward: Interact with the Word

For the word of God is living and active, sharper than any two-edged sword, piercing to the division of soul and of spirit, of joints and of marrow, and discerning the thoughts and intentions of the heart. Hebrews 4:12 ESV

The Word is alive! I want it to come alive to you! I want you to keep going with this journaling practice by writing Scripture.

Why write instead of just read? If I showed you a picture of a pot of geraniums with a butterfly on it, you might be able to name what was in the picture. But what if I took the picture away and asked you to draw it? Would you want to see the picture again before you drew it? Would you look more closely and observe more detail?
It's the same way when we write the Word; it often helps us pay attention to more detail!

How do you do this?
I do it by writing out a verse slowly while allowing the Holy Spirit to illuminate words or give me a picture of how it looks like in my life. Sometimes I even imagine myself there in Bible times as hearing it come from the author's mouth. I spend time with the Lord and the verse, letting it run through my mind, "chewing" on it so to speak.

Here's how it looks for me, I write the verse:
For we are God's handiwork, created in Christ Jesus to do good works, which God prepared in advance for us to do. Ephesians 2:10 NIV

Then I begin to write out the truths from the Scripture:
I am God's handiwork, His creation; He created me to do good things, I have purpose; Thank you Lord for my uniqueness; show me how to live out my purpose and do the good things you have planned for me; walk beside me through it all.

and finish by just talking to God, asking questions, praying and writing down whatever comes to mind.

Your words were found, and I ate them, and your words became to me a joy and the delight of my heart, for I am called by your name, O LORD, God of hosts. Jeremiah 15:16 ESV

Jeremiah received the Word like nourishing food. Let's savor His Word like Jeremiah!

Write out the following verses (on the next page) and spend some time with the Lord. Ask Him to show you the truth of His Word and how it applies to your life. Go slow, write out and journal one verse a day.
*1 Peter 4:10
Ephesians 2:10
Romans 12:1
1 Corinthians 10:31
Matthew 5:16*

Memorial Stones

Then Joshua called the twelve men whom he had appointed from the children of Israel, one man from every tribe; and Joshua said to them: "Cross over before the ark of the Lord your God into the midst of the Jordan, and each one of you take up a stone on his shoulder, according to the number of the tribes of the children of Israel, that this may be a sign among you when your children ask in time to come, saying, 'What do these stones mean to you?' Joshua 4:4-6 NKJV

At the end of each mission, I want you to write down your "memorial stones." Start by summarizing what the chapter was about and then add in what you learned in this mission? These "stones" act as reminders of God's faithfulness and will provide a testimony of all He has done in you when you end this journey.

Pile up your stones from Mission #1 now...

MISSION TWO
Discover a higher purpose for healthy

There are many reasons people chase health. Often, it's based on the outward appearance—wanting to look a certain way, preparing for a swimsuit or wedding gown. Others look at energy and their ability to do things they love, like tennis or running. Fewer look at long-term mobility and quality of life. Fewer still look at spiritual health.

I'm guessing you've tried various methods to improve your health before—some good and some not so good. We aren't going to focus on our wins or our failures. In this mission, I want you to examine your heart, talking to God and considering why health, peace and purpose is something you long for.

My reasons for pursuing "health" changed drastically after watching my father's four-year battle with cancer. It's rough to watch someone slowly die from a chronic illness. Cancer treatment aims for the five-year mark to achieve "survivor" status. It fails to care about the "survivors" quality of life! As prolific as cancer is, I'm sure you too have witnessed the brutality of the treatment and how it sucks the life right out of the patient.

After my father passed, I told someone that he had been alive but not living. I think that sums it up well. From that point on, I decided that I wanted to live all the days I was alive! I had witnessed one way to do life and decided that I wanted more; I wanted different.

This is when my searching led me to deep research into natural health protocols. Learning to battle cancer, one of the biggest chronic illnesses around, became my goal. I figured if I learned how to battle cancer, then I could battle anything. I'm embarrassed to say that I spent a lot of time researching all that could benefit the physical body, neglecting the internal—the things that would improve my spirit and soul's health where peace and purpose enter the equation.

Thankfully, God led me to upgrade my ambition several years ago. I don't always do a "word of the year," but as the new year started, I just kept seeing "shine" everywhere. I decided to chew on that word and let it be something I dwelt on and dug deeper into. By the end of the year, I really felt God saying that He didn't just call me to "live all the days you're alive" but to "live to shine" for Him. Now I didn't hear that in an audible voice, and not all at once, but it was a message that came at me through many avenues over the course of a few months. It was so loud that I knew that it must be Him!

Purpose for the Journey

In the same way, let your light shine before others, that they may see your good deeds and glorify your Father in heaven. Matthew 5:16 NIV

This verse in Matthew became my life verse after God upgraded my purpose to "live to shine" for Him. I know that if I'm shining for Him, I'm spreading His love to others.

You may think, "That's great for you Stephanie, but I don't feel called and I don't think I have what it takes." In Exodus chapters 3 and 4, Moses looks at his inadequacies instead of looking at God. He focuses so much on his own shortcomings that he doesn't think God can use him. Sounds sort of funny when you think about it. The God of the Universe, who created the world, can't make Moses speak eloquently or be the leader God called him to be—Crazy talk!

God uses yielded people to be His hands and feet. God says HE is going to rescue the Israelites (Exodus 3:8) but he sent a person. He sent Moses. Moses was part of God's rescue plan! God uses people as the vehicle for His love. YOU, my friend, are also a container and a vehicle of His love! This is a higher purpose for being healthy!

Exodus 3:11 But Moses said to God, "Who am I..."
Are you saying the same thing to God, "Who am I to do anything for you?"

If you aren't familiar with the story, Moses fled to a foreign land because he killed a man. And you know what? That didn't disqualify him! His heart yearned for justice for his people—he just took care of it all wrong. But with God, Moses became the one to lead the people out of slavery into a new land. God isn't looking for perfect people, He's used many types of people in the past, a coward (Gideon), a prostitute (Rahab), and murderers (Moses and David). He's used the old (Abraham) and the young (Timothy). None of those things disqualified them!

He's looking for those that are willing! He's looking for those that say YES! (Did you say YES to him from the last mission?)

God takes the ordinary and He makes the extraordinary take place WITH HIM and His power at work through them—that's living on purpose!

Your eyes saw my unformed substance; in your book were written, every one of them, the days that were formed for me, when as yet there was none of them. Psalm 139:16 ESV

God knew you would be here right now in this year, in this country, in this culture. Just as Mordecai reminded Esther, I remind you:

And who knows whether you have not come to the kingdom for such a time as this? Esther 4:14b

You have purpose! You can be God's love in your unique way to those God has called you to—but not if you are too sick, too weak, too defeated.

Choose to walk in vibrant health, rise to the challenge like Esther and live on purpose!

Possible Obstacles on Your Journey
Remember I said I don't want you just reading this book for knowledge? This is a book for you to use to partner with God and let Him transform you. So be willing to say "Yes" and then GO! Do the next right thing that you feel He is calling you to do.

In each mission we'll look at steps we can take to give God the space, time, and obedience He needs to transform us. We'll also look at possible obstacles that may be blocking our way. So, when you get to a possible obstacle, work through the exercise, and clear the blockage so you can continue traveling on your journey.

Expect that working through the obstacles requires time with your Father and His Word. Relationships take time, and it's no different with Him. I know I had lots of excuses for not devoting time to Him, which mostly involved raising five kids. But when life got too hard to handle, I read my Bible more and kept the praise music playing. I soaked it all in—I had to, because it became my lifeline when life felt like it was falling apart. Unfortunately, we often wait until the hard times come before we press into God. I pray you'll take every opportunity to press in when it's not hard, so you'll be prepared when the hard hits!

Check for Obstacle

Read Exodus chapters 3 and 4. Consider Moses' question, "Who am I...?" Have you been saying the same thing to God?

What lies are you believing about yourself? In what ways are you disqualifying yourself? The lies you believe are obstacles that need to be removed to continue on the journey. Spend time with these questions, journal and talk to God as you do this next "Go Forward" activation.

Go Forward: Interact with the Word
Peace comes as we believe we are who God says we are, and we can live life with purpose. Write out the following verses and spend time with the Lord. Ask Him to show you the truth of His Word and how it applies to the purpose of pursuing health.

Remember, slow is better, maybe just take one verse a day until you complete the list to give God time to speak to you. We are not just checking boxes off our to-do list; we want to allow the Word to penetrate and change our hearts.

John 15:16
1 Corinthians 3:16
Esther 4:14
1 Corinthians 9:24
Mark 12:30-31

Choose to Run Your Race

No, I'm not asking you to run an actual race! But I want you to consider your purpose on this earth as a race like Paul described in the New Testament:

Therefore, since we are surrounded by so great a cloud of witnesses, let us also lay aside every weight, and sin which clings so closely, and let us run with endurance the race that is set before us, looking to Jesus, the founder and perfecter of our faith, who for the joy that was set before him endured the cross, despising the shame, and is seated at the right hand of the throne of God. – Hebrews 12:1-2 ESV

Do you not know that in a race all the runners run, but only one receives the prize? So run that you may obtain it. 1 Corinthians 9:24 ESV

And knowing death was coming soon, Paul told Timothy:
I have fought the good fight, I have finished the race, I have kept the faith.
2 Timothy 4:7 ESV

You too have a race to run!
What's this race about? It's about living on purpose—running your race and hearing "Well done, good and faithful servant." (Matthew 25:23)

Check for an Obstacle

Where there is no vision, the people perish: but he that keepeth the law, happy is he. Proverbs 29:18 KJV

The remaining missions in this book are the HOW. They will walk you down the path to becoming a woman of vibrant health that walks in peace and purpose. But if we don't know WHY, what does the HOW matter?! In fact, I would say that many of us know the how, but we lack the WHY to give us the motivation to DO the how.

For example: Do you know you should floss your teeth every day? Do you?

So, what you need is not information for how to do it—you need the motivation to do it. You need a WHY big enough to help you with motivation.

Go Forward: Write Your Vision for Vibrant Health
So why do you want to be healthy? Why do you want to walk in peace and purpose? To get at the deeper root meaning for you, ask yourself "why?" five times (or more if needed).

You'll answer the first time, then ask, "Why that?" and for each answer—ask WHY again? Keep asking WHY until you get at the answer that pulls at your heart. Use the space on the next page or in your own journaling notebook.
Consider: Why health? Why peace and purpose?

My Example:
Why do I want to get healthy?
I want to feel good & have energy

Why do you want to feel good & have energy?
I want to feel good & have the energy to do the things I want

Why do you want to be able to do the things you want?
I don't ever want sickness to keep me from enjoying life

Why do you want to avoid sickness and enjoy life?
I want to be able to enjoy life with hubby, kids, & grandkids and not held back by sickness

Why do you want to be able to enjoy life with them?
Because I saw how sickness robbed life from my father and I want to enjoy life with my family. I want to have energy and feel good so I can live out my purpose as long as God allows me days on this earth.

Look at your answers to the first question and to the fifth question. Compare how you feel after reading the fifth to how you feel reading the first. There's no magic about five. You could keep digging and ask a couple more times. Your goal is to get to the answer that makes you smile or start to tear up. Because when you get to the answer that causes emotion, you know you are getting to the root motivation.

You can repeat the exercise with peace and purpose as well. "What would my life look like if I walked full of peace and purpose?"

Go Forward: What's Your Higher Purpose for Vibrant Health?
Now I invite you to take this all to God. Does He have more to say on this? Does He want to upgrade it? Be sure to write down all your thoughts and prayers. You will want to remember it when days get hard, when it seems overwhelming and when you've lost direction.

Now it's time to write down your "memorial stones." Summarize this mission. What truths has God shown you? These "stones" act as reminders of God's faithfulness and will provide a testimony of all He has done in you.

Pile up your stones from Mission #2 now...

MISSION THREE
Work inside out

Woe to you, scribes and Pharisees, hypocrites! For you clean the outside of the cup and the plate, but inside they are full of greed and self-indulgence. You blind Pharisee! First clean the inside of the cup and the plate, that the outside also may be clean. Matthew 23:25-26 ESV

The Pharisees loved their rules. Here in Matthew, we see Jesus' rebuke and how He implores them to pay more attention to what's on the inside.

The law given in the Old Testament was an outside-in approach and a weak substitute for what we have now, Jesus Christ, the new covenant. So now, if you are a believer, you have the Holy Spirit living in you! Our focus should shift from the flesh to the internal Spirit living inside us.

For to set the mind on the flesh is death but to set the mind on the Spirit is life and peace. Romans 8:6 ESV

Do you not know that you are God's temple and that God's Spirit dwells in you? 1 Corinthians 3:16 ESV

What you'll see most in this mission was something I learned slowly and over five years.

This quote by Sherrie Rice Smith from "EFT for Christians" sums up this mission:

"It is very difficult to experience health in our body if we are broken emotionally or spiritually. Our body is an outer reflection and expression of the inner health of our soul." [2]

I witnessed this right after I finished my naturopath training and began to see clients. I saw clients that wanted me to help them avoid or trade out their prescriptions for an herb or supplement. As we talked, my spirit was stirred with compassion because I saw that they needed inner healing and help that comes from Jesus, not a pill or the perfect diet. Later I experienced this myself as well. Stuffing emotions, I tried to push through until my physical body was worn and stressed to exhaustion.

Thankfully, God brought many great resources to me and showed me insight through His Word. I journaled and drew pictures that helped me understand the principle of working inside out. It started simply with some circles and a heart in the center, but as I kept growing and learning, God kept refining it. Even today, I tend to see things as extensions or 3D representations of this God-given model that I'm sharing with you.

The Vibrant Health Framework™
As I began to read and learn more and more about natural health from a biblical viewpoint, this picture (next page) began to evolve. I love that the Lord helps me understand things with pictures! It's my hope that this picture He showed me will help you understand as well.

I like definitions—they ensure that you and the person you are talking with are on the same page. So, let's look at some definitions from the 1828 Webster's Dictionary:

   Vibrant = pulsating with life, vigor, or activity
   Health = the condition of being sound in body, mind, or spirit
   Framework = a skeletal or structural framework

So, the Vibrant Health Framework™ is the structure we use to be sound in body, mind and spirit seen as pulsating with life, vigor, and activity. It becomes part of the end goal of our journey.

Does this resonate with your "why" (mission #2)?

Starts with Vertical Relationship
And they said, "Believe in the Lord Jesus, and you will be saved, you and your household." Acts 16:31 ESV

The moment you believed in the Lord Jesus Christ, when God's light and love poured into your heart, you became a new creation! God filled you up from the inside!

Our Vibrant Health Framework™ has a heart at the center that is signifying the saving work of Christ.

You can see my journal drawing showing His Spirit coming from heaven filling my spirit. This vertical relationship with God must be the starting point for true Vibrant Health! We align everything from positioning God first.

God is the Fountain of Life
You need the God of love to fill you completely to be able to live on purpose.

On the last day of the feast, the great day, Jesus stood up and cried out, "If anyone thirsts, let him come to me and drink. Whoever believes in me, as the Scripture has said, 'Out of his heart will flow rivers of living water.'" John 7:37-38 ESV

Are you thirsty for more of God's presence? More of His living water flowing through you?

May the God of hope fill you with all joy and peace in believing, so that by the power of the Holy Spirit you may abound in hope. Romans 15:13 ESV

For with you is the fountain of life; in your light do we see light. Psalm 36:9 ESV

I know you've heard the saying, "You can't pour from an empty cup." We know it's true and yet we try to fill ourselves in so many other ways. We push through until exhaustion, then we get up and do it again day after day. But what if we let the Lord fill us up from the inside, rippling through our soul and then out through our body? What would life look like if we lived inside out?

For God, who said, "Let light shine out of darkness," has shone in our hearts to give the light of the knowledge of the glory of God in the face of Jesus Christ. 2 Corinthians 4:6 ESV

Go Forward: Interact with the Word

The Word is an abundant well you can go to for all things. Please don't tire of studying His Word. Psalm 36:5-9 is a rich passage for you to focus on at this time. Write it out, meditate and pray on it, and then journal your revelations.

Triune Beings

As we explore the framework further, we need to look at another truth: Man as a triune being like his Creator. You have a spirit, a soul, and a physical body, represented by three concentric circles in the picture. I believe God cares about all three parts and we shouldn't stop at salvation of the spirit and exclude the soul and body.

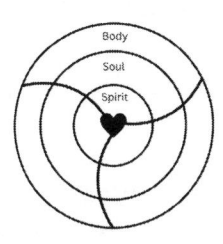

Throughout the Bible we can find many verses that speak to people as having these three parts, like my favorite from Mark:

And you shall love the Lord your God with all your heart and with all your soul and with all your mind and with all your strength. Mark 12:30 ESV

Reflect on that verse in combination with this verse:

Now may the God of peace himself sanctify you completely, and may your whole spirit and soul and body be kept blameless at the coming of our Lord Jesus Christ. 1 Thessalonians 5:23 ESV

Webster's Dictionary 1828 says "sanctify" means to separate, set apart or appoint to a holy, sacred, or religious use.

The prayer and desire of Paul in 1 Thessalonians is that God would sanctify every part of your being—spirit, soul, and body. The Vibrant Health Framework™ is a picture of this process of sanctification in all three parts of you. Graphically, it shows the three parts drawn as concentric circles from the inside out, starting with the spirit. Internally, in the spirit and soul, is where we find ourselves loving God and ourselves. Then when we choose to love others, the physical body is the vehicle we use.

Read this quote by Sherrie Rice Smith again:
"It is very difficult to experience health in our body if we are broken emotionally or spiritually. Our body is an outer reflection and expression of the inner health of our soul."

Looking at our definitions of vibrant health and considering three parts of us, ask yourself:
  Is your spirit energetic and full of life?
  Is your soul (your mind, will & emotions) pulsating with life?
  And lastly, would you say your physical body is pulsating with vigor and energy?

I do believe it's possible to live an abundant and vibrant life in Christ! This Vibrant Health Framework™ puts everything into proper alignment. It helps you see where to start and where to go. It's the structure you can use on your own journey to become a healthy Vibrant Woman. When we get off balance, our focus on God can restore healthy alignment.

Go Forward: Interact with the Word

We often need to renew our mind and dig deeper to solidify truth in our own minds. I'd like for you to write out the Word and 'chew' on the words, circle them, draw pictures around them in whatever creative way God brings to you. Let the Word come alive!

Spend time dwelling on Psalm 103:1-5 and consider what it says or how it references you as a triune being and note the blessings that it lists and how those affect each part of you.

Check for a Roadblock

Let's come back to a verse from the beginning of this mission:

For to set the mind on the flesh is death but to set the mind on the Spirit is life and peace. Romans 8:6 ESV

Are you working outside-in?
What are you pushing and striving for?
Do you have "life and peace"?
What have you set your mind on?
What does it look like to be focused on the flesh?

It could mean we look to the body to comfort us with food or fitting into those jeans. It could mean we get our confidence in finishing that workout or the reflection we see in the mirror. It could also look like shame when we don't like what we see. It could mean dressing up the outside to mask the mess on the inside. How does it look in your life? Pride or shame are two indicators that tell us that we've made it all about us and not about God.

Paul tells us in Romans 8 that the law was an outside-in, flesh-focused approach that was weak. Thankfully, the new law, the law of the Spirit in Christ, sets us free!

For the law of the Spirit of life has set you free in Christ Jesus from the law of sin and death. Romans 8:2 ESV

Go Forward: Interact with the Word

Commit to reading and meditating on Romans 8:1-17 for several days. Read it each day and ask God to reveal more about the Holy Spirit and the difference you see in inside-out living versus outside-in living. Be sure to journal your new revelations!

Romans 8:1-17

Rest to Refill

Come to Me, all you who are weary and burdened, and I will give you rest. Take My yoke upon you and learn from Me; for I am gentle and humble in heart, and you will find rest for your souls. For My yoke is easy and My burden is light. Matthew 11:28-30 NIV

Jesus said His burden is light, His yoke easy. Juggling little ones, taxiing kids around, financial pressures and just life—did not always feel light or easy to me. The more I was striving, the less peaceful I was. Can you relate?

Fixing our eyes on God and getting back in alignment with Him is simple but not always easy. It requires us to get still.

Be still, and know that I am God. I will be exalted among the nations, I will be exalted in the earth! Psalm 46:10 ESV

When the pandemic of 2020 shut down life and locked us up at home, I found something that showed me the value in getting still with God. I signed up for some online classes where we moved, breathed, meditated on the Word, and got still with God. It was life-giving to me! I felt reconnected to God in the stillness, and I began to truly receive and know His love.

I witnessed a similar phenomenon happening when homeschooling my boys. Getting the boys to sit and get schoolwork done was not always easy. On many occasions I had them get up and go outside and run around the house a few times to burn off some energy so they could come in and sit down. It usually worked wonderfully!

Having experienced for myself, I now see the beauty in moving and then having a greater capacity to sit in stillness with the Lord.

Go Forward: Walk and Be Still

I propose that you put some headphones on, turn up the worship music and go for a walk. It doesn't have to be a race, just walk for maybe 15 minutes. Let your mind focus on the worship music as you move. Then give yourself five to ten minutes to sit still with the music off.

You don't need to fill the silence with talking, but sit, listen, and know Him. Consider the music you just heard. Maybe sit and enjoy His creation. Just listen. God wants a relationship with you and He's waiting for you to draw near. Take a notebook and write out what you are feeling and what you are sensing from the Spirit.

But he would withdraw to desolate places and pray. Luke 5:16 ESV

Jesus would often remove himself from the chaos of the world to get quiet and spend time in fellowship with the Father. Shouldn't we also do the same?

I wish I could say that the more I did this the easier it became, but it's still a discipline. It's so true that the enemy will try to keep us busy and distracted. But press in and do it again and again! God always refreshes and renews when I stop and get still.

We are just getting started on this journey. It seems like small steps right now, but in the end, I believe you will see the value in this Vibrant Health Framework™, living inside-out. The journey to becoming a vibrant woman will flow naturally when you stay in alignment with your Father.

What "memorial stones" are you walking out of this mission with? Summarize and record your "stones" so you'll have a reminder of God's faithfulness.

Pile up your stones from Mission #3 now…

MISSION FOUR
Embrace the process for transformation

In the last mission, we established that we are working inside out. We've also looked at our personal reasons why we are pursuing health. Now let's dig a little more into transformation.

Transformation is bigger than any before-and-after photo you've seen on your Facebook newsfeed. It's bigger than wanting to fit into that swimsuit before your vacation. It's bigger than setting out to run a 5K.

In Romans, it tells us to "be transformed."

Do not conform to the pattern of this world, but be transformed by the renewing of your mind. Then you will be able to test and approve what God's will is—his good, pleasing and perfect will. Romans 12:2 NIV

These two verses give us a little more...

Therefore, if anyone is in Christ, the new creation has come: The old has gone, the new is here! 2 Corinthians 5:17 NIV

For this is the will of God, your sanctification... 1 Thessalonians 4:3a NKJV

Webster's Dictionary 1828 says "sanctification" is the act of consecrating or of setting apart for a sacred purpose.

Transformation is the process of sanctification, of being set apart, and stepping into the "new creation" 2 Corinthians says you have become in Christ.

Invited into the Transformation Process

For we are God's fellow workers. You are God's field, God's building.
1 Corinthians 3:9 ESV

God woos you as He calls you to Him, and his wooing doesn't end at salvation. God is calling you now to co-labor with Him, to be His partner. Just as God invited Moses to be His spokesperson and free the Israelites (Exodus 3). As God asked the Israelites to march around Jericho seven times and then shout (Joshua 6). And as Naaman was asked to wash in the Jordan river seven times (2 Kings 5). In these instances, God himself was responsible for the powerful outcomes but He invited these men to partner with Him.

When we say yes to Jesus and the salvation He offers — is transformation instantaneous? No, it's not. This is where co-laboring comes into play. The opportunity before you now, will you partner with God? Will you co-labor with Him and stop going it alone?

As I sat with this truth, I decided to search the Word and renew my mind about what the Lord was asking of me. I started making a simple list. I quickly filled the back and front of a page before I decided to stop.

Here's just a small sampling of things I found that I was to do as a partner of the Lord:
- Renew your mind, Romans 12:1-2
- Take every thought captive, 2 Corinthians 10:3-5
- Repent and be baptized, Acts 2
- Confess our sins, 1 John 1:8-10
- Hide God's Word, Psalm 119:11
- Walk in the Spirit, Galatians 5
- Delight yourself in the Lord, Psalm 37:4
- Rejoice always, pray without ceasing, 1 Thessalonians 5:16-18
- Abide in Jesus, John 15:5
- Stand firm, Ephesians 6:11
- Be imitators of God, Ephesians 5:1
- Seek first His Kingdom, Matthew 6:33
- Trust in the Lord, Psalm 37:3

From all that I was reading, it seemed clear that I was not to just sit around waiting for God to transform me. No, we all need to actively live out our faith.

Let the one who is taught the word share all good things with the one who teaches. Do not be deceived: God is not mocked, for whatever one sows, that will he also reap. For the one who sows to his own flesh will from the flesh reap corruption, but the one who sows to the Spirit will from the Spirit reap eternal life. Galatians 6:6-8 ESV

We need to be intentional about what we are sowing to see the transformation we desire! That's why we have the "3 C's" process to help us on our journey to vibrant health.

Cleanse, Cultivate, Continue
Let me first explain how I came to these three C's. It all started because I was looking at ways to cancer-proof my life early in my studies.

I came across the book, "Never Be Sick Again" by Raymond Francis. The catchy title packs a big promise, and I was intrigued! Like I said, I like simplicity, and this author really simplified things. He said ultimately there was just one disease, malfunctioning cells. He blamed this single disease on two causes, toxicity and deficiency.
Is this oversimplified? Perhaps, but what it does is force you to look for root causes.

Are you lacking something you need? Then you are deficient.
Do you have things that you don't need? Then you are toxic.

Looking at root cause instead of mounting an attack against symptoms is heralded in the natural health world. Modern Western medicine is, however, all about symptom management.

Looking at deficiency and toxicity, can you see why natural health practitioners are pushing detoxes and nutritional supplements? I've been one of them too! When we can correct these two things, the body begins to work just as God designed it to work! I took these two negatives, toxicity and deficiency, and flipped them into positives: cleanse and cultivate. Then I added a third one, continue. This is a brief introduction to our three steps that we'll use throughout all our remaining missions.

Step #1 - Cleanse
Consider toxicity and the opposite, which is to "cleanse."

Cleanse = to purify; to make clean; to remove filth
It's the process of getting rid of what we don't need or what doesn't serve us.

We see this in the Bible with our spiritual health:
Therefore if anyone cleanses himself from the latter, he will be a vessel for honor, sanctified and useful for the Master, prepared for every good work. 2 Timothy 2:21 NKJV

If we confess our sins, He is faithful and righteous to forgive us our sins and to cleanse us from all unrighteousness. 1 John 1:9 ESV

And in spiritual and physical health:
Therefore, since we have these promises, dear friends, let us purify ourselves from everything that contaminates body and spirit, perfecting holiness out of reverence for God. 2 Corinthians 7:1 NIV

Process one is about cleansing your spirit, soul, and physical body.

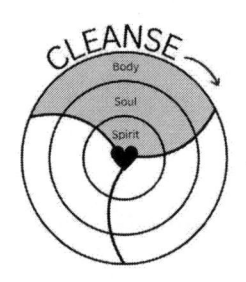

When we look at the Vibrant Health Framework™, we see the swirls that are circling clockwise—these are the 3 C's of cleanse, cultivate and continue. The shaded area represents "Cleanse," and you can see that it overlaps spirit, soul, and body. It overlaps because we need to cleanse each part of us to attain the transformation we long for.

Step #2 - Cultivate
Francis' second cause of disease is deficiency, which means there are things you need to operate and be "healthy" that you currently lack. Let's look at the positive side which I am calling the second process, "cultivate."

Cultivate = to till; to prepare for crops; to foster the growth of

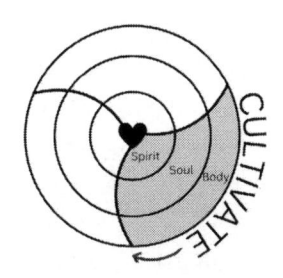

"Cultivate" is all about fostering growth by supplying what's needed in your spirit, in your soul and in your physical body. Again, it overlaps spirit, soul, and body because the work of cultivating needs to happen in all three areas.

Step #3 - Continue
That brings us to step number three: "continue."

Continue = to remain in a state or place; to maintain without interruption a condition, course, or action

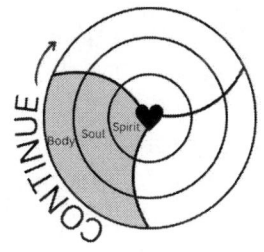

This is the commitment to continue yielding your body (all of you) to God's calling and continuing your journey, to continue to grow and bear fruit. You are abiding in Him and giving Him the space and obedience He needs.

I'm going to offer these verses from the Passion Translation because it explains step three so well.

So then, refuse to answer [sin's] call to surrender your body as a tool for wickedness. Instead, passionately answer God's call to keep yielding your body to him as one who has now experienced resurrection life! You live now for his pleasure, ready to be used for his noble purpose. Romans 6:13 TPT

In the same way you received Jesus our Lord and Messiah by faith, continue your journey of faith, progressing further into your union with him! Colossians 2:6 TPT

Jesus was our perfect example of yielding to the Father.
For I have come down from heaven, not to do my own will but the will of him who sent me. John 6:38 ESV

That day that I rushed out of my house, heart racing, a knot in my stomach with a need to run away—I had to surrender and yield! I knew that I had been holding on so tight; and that I just couldn't do it anymore. God showed me that I had to surrender my expectations of the outcome. Because the more I held on to my expectations, the more anxiety arose. To "continue" in what I knew to be true meant I had to yield and rest in Him. When we yield to His outcomes, we can stop striving and trying to control everything.

Stop striving and know that I am God; I will be exalted among the nations, I will be exalted on the earth. Psalm 46:10 NASB

Stop for Warning Signal
Have you said to yourself something along these lines...
- This all hinges on me.
- I'm in control.
- I just need to work harder.
- I can make this happen.

I grew up with a very independent spirit and I was a firm believer in self-reliance! I also praised it when I saw it in my own children. But later, I realized that it made having a relationship with the Lord very difficult. I was so self-reliant that I found it very hard to trust and surrender to Him.

The truth is, you can't be in a relationship and partnership with someone if you don't trust them. I had to confess so I could yield and surrender. Check your own heart for similar mindsets that indicate that you've not partnered with the Lord and are trying to go it alone.

No more lone-ranger spirit—cleanse by confessing the lies you've been believing, cultivate by renewing your mind with Scripture, and continue to yield every time these lies start to rear their ugly head.

Now to Him who is able to do far more abundantly beyond all that we ask or think, according to the power that works within us, Ephesians 3:20 NASB

God wants to be our strength in all things. Embrace these processes as you lay the outcomes up to Him.

Go Forward: Interact with the Word
John chapter 15 is a good example of the processes of cleanse, cultivate and continue. Spend time reading and talking to God about John 15 regarding health in spirit, soul, and body.

I've included this chapter from the Passion translation for you to mark up on the next two pages. Grab some colored pens, pencils, markers.... select one color for cleanse, one for cultivate and one for continue. Highlight phrases and words that indicate one of these steps is being taken. Then notice the result of these processes and select a color for that as well.

Write down all the things God reveals from this chapter.

LIVE IN VIBRANT HEALTH

John 15:1-17 The Passion Translation

1 *"I am a true sprouting vine, and the farmer who tends the vine is my Father.*

2 *He cares for the branches connected to me by lifting and propping up the fruitless branches and pruning every fruitful branch to yield a greater harvest.*

3 *The words I have spoken over you have already cleansed you.*

4 *So you must remain in life-union with me, for I remain in life-union with you. For as a branch severed from the vine will not bear fruit, so your life will be fruitless unless you live your life intimately joined to mine.*

5 *"I am the sprouting vine and you're my branches. As you live in union with me as your source, fruitfulness will stream from within you—but when you live separated from me you are powerless.*

6 *If a person is separated from me, he is discarded; such branches are gathered up and thrown into the fire to be burned.*

7 *But if you live in life-union with me and if my words live powerfully within you—then you can ask whatever you desire and it will be done.*

8 *When your lives bear abundant fruit, you demonstrate that you are my mature disciples who glorify my Father!*

9 *"I love each of you with the same love that the Father loves me. You must continually let my love nourish your hearts.*

10 *If you keep my commands, you will live in my love, just as I have kept my Father's commands, for I continually live nourished and empowered by his love.*

11 *My purpose for telling you these things is so that the joy that I experience will fill your hearts with overflowing gladness!*

12 *"So this is my command: Love each other deeply, as much as I have loved you.*

13 *For the greatest love of all is a love that sacrifices all. And this great love is demonstrated when a person sacrifices his life for his friends.*

14 *"You show that you are my intimate friends when you obey all that I command you.*

15 *I have never called you 'servants,' because a master doesn't confide in his servants, and servants don't always understand what the master is doing. But I call you my most intimate and cherished friends, for I reveal to you everything that I've heard from my Father.*

16 *You didn't choose me, but I've chosen and commissioned you to go into the world to bear fruit. And your fruit will last, because whatever you ask of my Father, for my sake, he will give it to you!*

17 *So this is my parting command: Love one another deeply!"*

What "memorial stones" are you walking out of this mission with? Summarize and record your "stones" so you'll have a reminder of God's faithfulness.

Pile up your stones from Mission #4 now...

MISSION FIVE
Connect with the heart of God

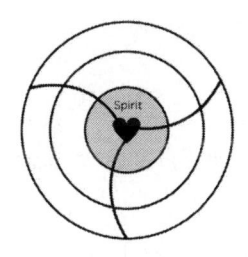

In mission #3 we established that we work inside-out on our journey. In this mission we focus on the spirit. Specifically, we look at ways we can connect with the heart of God. It's about building a relationship that will sustain us through the storms and help us live the vibrant life that shines. It's also about making the move from religion to relationship. Religion is an outside-in approach where we follow the rules and check all the boxes. Relationship is about knowing the Father, about receiving His love, and loving Him back.

Know Him

Not everyone who says to me, 'Lord, Lord,' will enter the kingdom of heaven, but the one who does the will of my Father who is in heaven. On that day many will say to me, 'Lord, Lord, did we not prophesy in your name, and cast out demons in your name, and do many mighty works in your name?' And then will I declare to them, 'I never knew you; depart from me, you workers of lawlessness.'
Matthew 7:21-23 ESV

Let us know; let us press on to know the LORD. Hosea 6:3a ESV

Be still, and know that I am God. I will be exalted among the nations, I will be exalted in the earth! Psalm 46:10 ESV

You have said, "Seek my face." My heart says to you, "Your face, LORD, do I seek."
Psalm 27:8 ESV

And my holy name I will make known in the midst of my people Israel, and I will not let my holy name be profaned anymore. And the nations shall know that I am the LORD, the Holy One in Israel. Ezekiel 39:7 ESV

God wants to know you and be known by you!

Check for Obstacle
Merriam-Webster defines legalism as "strict, literal, or excessive conformity to the law or to a religious or moral code."

The Pharisees loved their religious rules and traditions but missed the heart connection with God. Matthew 23 speaks of their outward obedience but inward waywardness. They missed out on relationship because of legalism.

Then they said to Moses, "Speak to us yourself and we will listen; but let not God speak to us, or we will die." Exodus 20:19 NASB

The Israelites weren't any better; they were fearful and asked for rules instead of relationship. Ouch!

What might it look like to be "religious" or "legalistic"? To be concerned more with the external than the internal relationship?

Here are a few observations about someone who is focused more on religion than relationship:
- Holds tight to traditions
- Fears new or different
- Compares, which often brings competition and division
- Dismisses the work of Holy Spirit
-Tries hard to look good to others
- Often tells themselves they "should do…"
- Easily offended and battles unforgiveness
- Does things out of obligation
- Critical or judgmental of others

As you read these, did any of them trigger offense? It could be an indicator that you need to examine your heart. They may show that you have focused on the external and missed the internal, heart connection. It can also mean you've been focused on yourself and what you could control.

Cleanse:
Ask the Lord if you need to cleanse yourself of some wrong thinking or actions.

If so, here's an example prayer:
Lord, forgive me for not giving you the opportunity to speak and for striving after my religious rules. Forgive me for refusing to hear You speak. Forgive me for putting myself at the center and being easily offended. I choose relationship over religion and rules. Please draw my heart near to You into a loving, intimate relationship.

Check for Obstacle
Behold what manner of love the Father has bestowed on us, that we should be called children of God! 1 John 3:1a NKJV

God is a good and loving Father. Unfortunately, we have earthly fathers that jade our view of our Heavenly Father and affect our relationship with Him.
How was your relationship with your earthly father (or even with a "father figure")? Whether you rate him good, awful, or evil, we have to accept that our Heavenly Father is different. Do you need to cleanse and cultivate a new view of who God the Father truly is so that you can be known and loved by Him?

Go Forward: Interact with the Word
Make Psalm 63:1 the cry of your own heart—tell Him now what's on your heart.

"O God, you are my God; earnestly I seek you; my soul thirsts for you; my flesh faints for you, as in a dry and weary land where there is no water." Psalm 63:1 ESV

Write Psalm 63:1-8 as a prayer to the Lord - or use it as inspiration to write a personalized prayer.

Psalm 63:1-8

Two Truths to Grasp
There are two truths that drastically changed my personal relationship with God. I want to share them because they helped me get past obstacles in my own journey. Maybe you have already experienced these truths, but I don't want to skip this because it was so important to my own journey. Once I experienced these, it changed the rhythms of my spiritual practices into enjoyable, uplifting times of transformation.

The first truth, if you are a believer of Christ, is that you always have the Holy Spirit with you as your helper, comforter, and guide. I knew this as a fact in my head from going to church, but I did not fully grasp it. Nor did I understand the power of the Holy Spirit. I was taught and led to believe the Spirit was quiet and no longer working and moving like He did in the Bible.

But that's not what the Bible says:
"Truly, truly, I say to you, whoever believes in me will also do the works that I do; and greater works than these will he do, because I am going to the Father. And I will ask the Father, and he will give you another Helper, to be with you forever, even the Spirit of truth, whom the world cannot receive, because it neither sees him nor knows him. You know him, for he dwells with you and will be in you. John 14:12, 16-17 ESV

Or do you not know that your body is a temple of the Holy Spirit within you, whom you have from God? 1 Corinthians 6:19a ESV

You, however, are not in the flesh but in the Spirit, if in fact the Spirit of God dwells in you. Anyone who does not have the Spirit of Christ does not belong to him. But if Christ is in you, although the body is dead because of sin, the Spirit is life because of righteousness. If the Spirit of him who raised Jesus from the dead dwells in you, he who raised Christ Jesus from the dead will also give life to your mortal bodies through his Spirit who dwells in you. Romans 8:9-11 ESV

Go Forward: Holy Spirit Study
When I realized that I had a messed-up view of the Holy Spirit I decided to go back to the Word. I needed to cleanse the wrong beliefs and cultivate my mind with The Truth. I

reread the New Testament and started a list of characteristics of the Holy Spirit. It didn't take long to realize how much I had missed my whole Christian life!

Maybe you need to renew your mind as well and you'd like to read through the New Testament, asking God to show you His Truth about the Holy Spirit. For now, I'd like you to start with these three chapters: Acts 2, Romans 8 and 1 Corinthians 12.
Be sure to journal all that you learn and hear from the Lord.

My sheep hear my voice, and I know them, and they follow me. - John 10:27 ESV

Secondly, because you have the Holy Spirit, believe that you can hear His voice. This was a huge revelation for me! I'm not sure how God led me to Mark Virkler but I watched some of his online videos. One included his testimony where He spoke of himself as analytical and religious and even admitted that he had been a "Pharisee." He had rejected all the "emotional experiential religious stuff" and stuck with only what his mind could analyze and figure out (very much like the Pharisees of Jesus' day.) I resonated with his story! He told how he had repented, and God transformed his religion into relationship—which is exactly what happened for me too! I purchased his book, "The 4 Keys to Hearing God's Voice." [3] I tried his method and was shocked how it improved my relationship and allowed me to get to know the Father in a much deeper way.

Check for Obstacle
Like Virkler, I had fallen into the trap of "rationalism." This obstacle takes a very cerebral outlook on life that relies solely on reason and knowledge. It involves using only the five senses to experience the natural world and thinking that's all there is. It partners well with legalism.

Could this be why Jesus said,

This is why I speak to them in parables: "Though seeing, they do not see; though hearing, they do not hear or understand. Matthew 13:13 NIV

In Acts 2 the body of believers were filled with the Holy Spirit causing them to speak in many different languages. The supernatural had taken place but there was a crowd to rationalize the experience.

Some, however, made fun of them and said,
"They have had too much wine." Acts 2:13 NIV

When have you rationalized the work of the Holy Spirit?
Confess and ask the Lord to continue to renew your mind and fill it with His Truth.

4 Keys to Hearing God

I'd like to share Virkler's four steps to hearing God's voice. (I must say that getting the book and watching his videos will take you much further, so I recommend them highly!)

Habakkuk 2:1-3 (NIV) are the verses Virkler uses to describe his process:

I will stand at my watch and station myself on the ramparts; I will look to see what he will say to me, and what answer I am to give to this complaint.
Then the Lord replied: "Write down the revelation and make it plain on tablets so that a herald may run with it. For the revelation awaits an appointed time; it speaks of the end and will not prove false. Though it linger, wait for it; it will certainly come and will not delay.

Four Keys to Hearing God's Voice:
1. Quiet yourself down to find the gentle voice of God (stand at my watch; station myself)
2. Fix your eyes on Jesus (look to see)
3. Tune to spontaneous thoughts (what he will say)
4. Write it down (write down the revelation)

He goes on to tell you how to do this practically and even gave a description I thought was very important. He says God's voice often comes as a spontaneous thought. A thought that comes suddenly. It's gentle and may be a picture, word, phrase, or impression.

Art Mathias of Wellspring Ministries says God can communicate differently to different people.[4] It may be a dream, vision, word picture, an impression, or a still small voice. But it can also be the pain in a memory is gone, a prompting to pray, a weight lifted, a release or peace from God. Don't expect it to look or be something specific.

The fourth key, "write it down," is super important! As soon as that spontaneous thought or feeling (or whatever!) comes, write it down. Don't stop to analyze it. Just write, and if it brings up a question or another thought, write that down. Then the next thought and the next thought, and so on.

If we don't write it down, our mind tends to rationalize and analyze the thought and dismiss the thought completely as our own thought. I tried this, just writing whatever popped into my brain. Surprisingly, I found that the journaling of any and all thoughts helped me distinguish my own thoughts from God speaking. Your thoughts tend to be analytical, but His thoughts are loving, gentle and spontaneous.

Virkler recommends having some spiritual advisors that can read over your writings as well. Again, the book is full of helpful information and helps to make sure you are hearing correctly. (For instance, knowing Scripture well to make sure what you hear doesn't contradict what God has already said is super important!)

One other note that helped me...
Every good thing given and every perfect gift is from above, coming down from the Father of lights, with whom there is no variation or shifting shadow.
James 1:17 NASB

I decided to shift my thinking and to thank God for every good thought and giving Him credit for every good thought I had. Through all this - God has really shown up for me! These things truly transformed my relationship with God. Guess what? He wants that same relationship with you too!

Go Forward: 4 Keys to Hearing God's Voice
Try this process for yourself. Picking a Scripture to write out is a helpful place to start. Pick out a Scripture now and walk through these steps as I describe how I do them (but it's not the only way!)

1. Quiet yourself down: I find an actual quiet space. If I don't have one, I put on headphones and play instrumental worship music to drown out other noise. I take a few deep breaths and invite the Lord to be near and for the Holy Spirit to open my spiritual ears to what He has to tell me.

2. Fix your eyes on Jesus: You can visualize this if it's helpful. Maybe you are sitting in front of Jesus' feet like Mary, soaking up all He is saying. Or you focus on the verses you wrote out or read. The Holy Spirit often seems to make a word or phrase stand out to me as I write that doesn't seem to happen when I just read. So, I let my focus be on the Scripture and the highlighted word or phrase.

3. Tune to spontaneous thoughts: This is where you must practice Psalm 46:10 (NASB) "Cease striving and know that I am God; I will be exalted among the nations, I will be exalted in the earth." This is where you sit and meditate and soak and let the Lord speak. Sometimes I ask a question: What does this word mean? What do You want me to know about this word/phrase? And I let thoughts flow.

4. Write it down: Whatever comes to mind, I write. It doesn't have to make sense or be in complete sentences: just write. I find writing also helps keep me focused and eliminates part of the chaos in my mind that can quickly detour me!

Give it a try now...but keep practicing, as it may not feel very comfortable at first. As you continue to sit with God, you'll nurture and grow your relationship.

___

___

___

___

___

___

___

___

___

___

___

Cultivate & Continue

Just like in our earthly relationships, building an intimate relationship with the Father requires time and intentionality. We can develop rhythms of spiritual practices that allow us to yield to the Father and cultivate that relationship that sanctifies and transforms. On our Vibrant Health Framework™, we are on the inside circle that represents our spirit. We've talked about cleansing some obstacles, now we look further as we cultivate and continue.

My favorite book on spiritual practices is "Sacred Rhythms" by Ruth Haley Barton.[5] We must understand that while we hunger for transformation, we aren't the one that is in charge of the finished outcome. What can we do? We can surrender and be intentional about making time and space for Holy Spirit to work and that's where spiritual practices come into play. We can easily fall into the trap of striving and trying to fix ourselves. There's a delicate balance of pursuing these spiritual practices and resting in the Lord.

Try out some Spiritual Practices

Barton's book includes a chapter on each of the following practices: solitude, Scripture, prayer, honoring the body, self-examination, discernment, and Sabbath. I highly encourage you to get the book—but I'd like to highlight a few key points as they relate to our journey of becoming vibrant women.

Solitude is a time we unplug and withdraw from the noise of life. Silence has been stolen from us; and we've allowed ourselves to be addicted to noise. Is it any wonder we feel disconnected from God?

"Be still, and know that I am God. I will be exalted among the nations, I will be exalted in the earth!" Psalm 46:10 ESV

The LORD will fight for you, and you have only to be silent. Exodus 14:14 ESV

For thus said the Lord GOD, the Holy One of Israel, "In returning and rest you shall be saved; in quietness and in trust shall be your strength." But you were unwilling, Isaiah 30:15 ESV

God is often heard in the still small voice, so we have to get away from the noise to hear Him.

And after the earthquake a fire, but the LORD was not in the fire; and after the fire a still small voice. 1 Kings 19:12 NKJV

Self-examination allows us to get honest with ourselves and is best done in solitude with God.

Search me, O God, and know my heart! Try me and know my thoughts! And see if there be any grievous way in me, and lead me in the way everlasting! Psalm 139:23-24 ESV

This time of self-examination allows us to be aware of God working in our lives and brings praise, worship, and gratitude. It also shows us our weaknesses and allows us time for confession and repentance.

Go Forward: Breath Prayer

Practicing a Breath Prayer can be helpful as you begin to pursue times of stillness and solitude. As I did this at a women's retreat, God showed me His love in such a sweet and tender way.

Why breath? Think about what your breathing pattern is like when you are:

    Mad = exaggerated forceful exhales

    Weeping, sad = spastic short inhales

    Fearful = tendency to hold our breath

Our breath is a unifying link between the physical, the spiritual, and the emotional.

Try it now:
- Close your eyes, place your hands on your navel or the top center of your chest
- Slow and steady let the belly fill

- As you inhale - pray a name for God (e.g., Abba Father)
- As you exhale - your personal short prayer (e.g., show me Your love for me)
- Keep repeating for several breaths and connect to the Lord

After you feel connection, continue to talk to God however you desire in that moment.

Inhale: _____

Exhale: _____

We've talked about our 3 C's: cleanse, cultivate and continue. "Cultivate" indicates fostering growth and this is most often done with spiritual practices. Typically, we would include prayer, reading the Word, fasting, meditation and worship here as well.

Read the Word: You know this discipline well but assess how you are reading. Consider—is it a time of seeking information or transformation? Are you stuck in that cerebral mindset, reading it like a textbook? Or are you reading a love letter? Ask God to allow your heart and soul to be penetrated by His intimate Word.

It is the Spirit who gives life; the flesh is no help at all. The words that I have spoken to you are spirit and life. John 6:63 ESV

As we read, it's natural to begin to pray and communicate with God. Let that flow! This can look like quiet thoughts to God, tears, groanings, singing and more. Let it be all that and more! Don't just check that reading list off for the day.

Honor God with your Body: In Sacred Rhythms, Barton explains that honoring the body is also a spiritual practice. That might be a new one for you, so I'd like to elaborate a bit.

"Or do you not know that your body is a temple of the Holy Spirit within you, whom you have from God? You are not your own" 1 Corinthians 6:19 ESV

Barton, "There is a very real connection between care for our body, our ability to continue deepening our relationship with God and our capacity to faithfully carry out God's purposes for our life over the long haul." I would agree!

After finishing training with Revelation Wellness and Holy Yoga, I realized how powerful it is to include the body into our spiritual life! This is also an area that Satan has twisted into glorifying the body. No, we are made to glorify God with our body. That's a huge difference!

Abiding: Our third "C" is for "Continue." This is a personal commitment to stay yielded to the Lord and continue the process of cleansing and cultivating, which is often called "abiding."

I am the vine; you are the branches. Whoever abides in me and I in him, he it is that bears much fruit, for apart from me you can do nothing. John 15:5 ESV

And Mary said, "Behold, I am the servant of the Lord; let it be to me according to your word." And the angel departed from her. Luke 1:38 ESV

"Let it be"… that is the confession of someone yielded to the will of the Father. She gave up her expectations and said yes to the outcome God had for her. Would you tell the Lord that right now?

Go Forward: Interact with the Word
Dig into Jeremiah 17:5-8. Write it, then chew on it, savor it, meditate on it, and then journal your revelations.

Consistency and Intentionality
Cultivating rhythms for spiritual transformation will require consistency and intentionality. Random and haphazard actions will give you random and haphazard results.

Ask God for guidance to develop a rhythm that meets your desire for life-giving connection with Him and spiritual transformation.

There are many options! You want to find a way that works for you—in your current season of life, with your personality and how you like building relationships. Don't compare your rhythms with someone else's but seek the Lord's desires for you. Commit to practicing intentionality in cleansing, cultivating, and continuing as you experiment and incorporate new spiritual practices with what you've done in the past.

Consider and journal:
· How do you want to live so you can be who you want to be?
· How can you make yourself available to God?
· What time and space will you give to Him?
· What needs to be removed to make this space?
· Will you let your time and attention be a gift to Him?

Whatever the Lord impresses on you, record it now as your "memorial stones." Your "memorial stones" are those things that you are walking out of that mission with that you've learned as truth. These "stones" act as reminders of God's faithfulness and will provide a testimony of all He has done for you.

Pile up your stones from Mission #5 now...

MISSION SIX

Come into agreement with the Father

"Knowing who you are has everything to do with how to live well." [6]
Alisa Keeton

I believe this quote from Alisa Keeton is seen played out in the movie Princess Diaries with Anne Hathaway and Julie Andrews. In the movie, Mia (Hathaway) finds out who she really is around her 15th birthday; she is actually a royal princess. Up to this point she thought she was a nobody. But then she meets the Queen of Genovia (Andrews) who calls her by her real name and title, saying "You are Amelia Mignonette Thermopolis Renaldi, Princess of Genovia." The movie shows Mia's journey of accepting her real identity and stepping into her purpose. That's what this mission is all about! I pray you finish this journey stepping into and believing who you are in Christ. Because at that point, you will begin to unlock joy, peace, and purpose.

Let's look at a couple of identity stories in the Bible:
I like Gideon's story in Judges 6 where he is hiding while threshing grain and in verse 12:
"And the angel of the Lord appeared to him and said to him, "The Lord is with you, O mighty man of valor." Judges 6:12 ESV

But at that moment, he was not acting like a "mighty man of valor" he was hiding. He comes across as weak and insignificant and then he argues with the angel:

And he said to him, "Please, Lord, how can I save Israel? Behold, my clan is the weakest in Manasseh, and I am the least in my father's house." Judges 6:15 ESV

"How can I…" Gideon only saw his weaknesses. In fact, he was rejecting his identity. Do you see that? In the movie, Mia also rejected her identity and wanted to continue playing small.

Thankfully, Gideon later chose to trust in God and agree with who God said he was, and God used him in a mighty way! He stepped into the identity that God gave him! (You can read Judges 6-8 for the full story.)

We see a similar situation with Moses in Exodus 3 when God called him from the burning bush. In verse 11, Moses responds to God, "Who am I..."? He was also rejecting his identity! In Exodus 3:8 (NIV), God told him, "I have come down to rescue them."

Who was going to rescue them? "I," that is "I AM."
God would be doing the work, and Moses was the vehicle God wanted to use. Where was Moses' focus? His focus was on himself, not on his Mighty God. When we are rejecting our identity, it's because we are so focused on our weaknesses and not in the Mighty God who is transforming us!

As you continue following Moses' story, you see him transform into a very capable leader. But he had to accept and take hold of his identity, and he needed to know and trust in God more to do it. Just like Moses, you will do and accomplish more when you take hold of your identity and believe in who God says you are. The more you know God and His nature, the more you'll trust in Him, and be able to live out your purpose.

Just like Gideon and Moses, Mia believed the lie that she was unimportant and a nobody. I can totally relate to Mia saying she tried to be invisible. In high school the last thing I wanted was to draw attention to myself. I didn't want to be seen so I tried very hard to stay small and blend in. When you try to play small, you deny who you are, rejecting your identity.

In my adult life, I've swung between playing small and going for big things. In this current season of writing a book, I've had to remind myself that to walk in Christ is to be holy, and that holy means to be set apart. It's going to look different than every other person and it's supposed to! I must keep my heart connected to Christ to keep the doubt at bay and stay on the right path.

Playing small and denying our identities leaves us feeling empty, and not ourselves. If you stay in that place, you will question anything you set out to do and often do nothing but stay stuck. It's a tiresome battle—a battle that God wants us all to be free of! Let's clean out all the old lies we've been carrying around.

Cleanse
The Lord has your identity already named. This mission is about using the 3C's to take your identity into your soul where you will "wear" it. You'll take hold of it and walk it out with purpose.

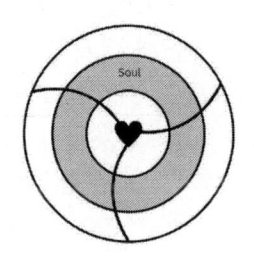

Our first step in the process is to stop and assess so that you can cleanse any lies that are causing you to reject your identity.

In the Garden, after Adam and Eve sinned, God asked them, "Who told you you were naked?" (Genesis 3:11)

How have you been rejecting your identity? What lies are you believing about yourself?

I want you to consider that first part, "Who told you...?"

Who told you....
  You aren't enough
  You are too shy
  You don't know enough
  You aren't anybody special
  You don't matter
  It's your fault
  You never do anything right
  You are worthless
....or any other lie you've been believing...

Revelation 12:10 calls Satan the "accuser" so yes, these are lies! We need to stop agreeing with the accuser.

"Awareness of a problem is the beginning of the solution." Dan Millman [7]

We can't correct what we fail to name. Stop now and consider the thoughts and lies that you say to yourself.

Go Forward: Truth Journaling
You can learn more about Truth Journaling in Barb Raveling's book, "The Renewing of the Mind Project."[8] But I'll share what she has on her blog to give you a general idea, because I believe this is enough for you to get started.

LIVE IN VIBRANT HEALTH

The goal with truth journaling is to take our thoughts captive. It's a practical application of:

For though we walk in the flesh, we do not war according to the flesh, for the weapons of our warfare are not of the flesh but divinely powerful for the destruction of fortresses. We are destroying speculations and every lofty thing raised up against the knowledge of God, and we are taking every thought captive to the obedience of Christ. 2 Corinthians 10:3-5 NKJV

Steps to truth journaling:
1. Begin by spilling your thoughts onto paper (no organizing or analyzing, just dump the thoughts you are having).
2. Number the different thoughts.
3. Look at each thought. Is it true or false? Consider Jesus standing in front of you, would He agree with what you've said about yourself?
4. Below your dump of thoughts, or on a clean sheet, write the truth for each corresponding thought. This may require a search for verses that will help you with this. (In her book, she gives you lists of verses for many possible negative thoughts.)
5. You may or may not want to save the original negative thoughts but save the list of God's truth so you can read over the list until you can walk in that identity.

During your self-evaluation you may realize there are some things you need to repent of. This is okay and good. Go ahead and ask God for forgiveness now. Also ask for forgiveness for coming into agreement with any lies. Specifically renounce those lies you were believing about yourself.

Example prayer:
Lord, forgive me for believing lies from the enemy. I confess, repent, and renounce the lie I've believed that I'm not enough (insert your lie). I am enough because You live in me! I choose to trust in Your Word and believe I am who You made me to be. In Jesus' name, I cancel all of Satan's authority over me because of this lie. Holy Spirit, heal my heart and speak words of truth to me.

Cultivate

In our transformational process, it is now time to "cultivate" and water our hearts. I invite you to discover who God says you are and envision yourself as the woman God sees. When we are confident in our identity in Christ, we will be better prepared to live on purpose.

In Jesus' day, every time someone said your name, they would be declaring your identity. I believe this speaks to how powerful our words are and how important our name is as well. Jacob meant "deceiver," and his life reflected that for many years. How would you feel if someone called you a deceiver all the time? Might that affect how you felt about yourself?

For as he thinks in his heart, so is he. Proverbs 23:7a NKJV

In Genesis 32, after wrestling with God, Jacob's name was changed to Israel. Israel means "contend with God." It expressed the concept of wrestling, clinging firmly to God, and overcoming. Jacob became an overcomer! So much different than 'deceiver'! God changed the names of several people in the Bible: Abram to Abraham; Saul to Paul; Simon to Peter, each time redeeming their identity.

To him the doorkeeper opens, and the sheep hear his voice; and he calls his own sheep by name and leads them out. John 10:3 NKJV

Your name also matters. What does your name mean? Have you looked it up?

More importantly, what does God call you? Is it different from your given name at birth? I was challenged to ask God what He called me….and God immediately dropped it into my heart, "Shining Light." It was a simple conversation with God that had a profound effect on me! I encourage you now to ask God what He calls you.

Jesus, our perfect example, knew who He was, and He knew His purpose.

Jesus said to them, "I am the bread of life; the one who comes to Me will not be hungry, and the one who believes in Me will never be thirsty. John 6:35 NASB

Again Jesus spoke to them, saying, "I am the light of the world. Whoever follows me will not walk in darkness, but will have the light of life." John 8:12 ESV

Jesus said to him, "I am the way, and the truth, and the life. No one comes to the Father except through me. John 14:6 ESV

But He said to them, "Let us go into the next towns, that I may preach there also, because for this purpose I have come forth." Mark 1:38 NKJV

God declared Jesus' identity:
And the Holy Spirit descended in bodily form like a dove upon Him, and a voice came from heaven which said, "You are My beloved Son; in You I am well pleased." Luke 3:22 NKJV

Satan, the accuser, tempted Jesus, a story you may know. Did you realize it was a test of His identity?

"If You are the Son of God, command that these stones become bread."
"If You are the Son of God, throw Yourself down."
"All these things I will give You if You will fall down and worship me."
Matthew 4:3, 6, 9 NKJV

This would all require Him to reject His identity.

Go Forward: Interact with the Word
Who does God say you are? The following list is a starting place for you to dig into the Word and write out what God has said. Write out one or two words that describe the attributes you see in these verses. It could be the actual word used in the verse or a word that conveys a similar meaning. Feel free to find other Scriptures as well.

Psalm 139:14 _____
Psalm 100:3 _____
Isaiah 49:16 _____
Isaiah 64:8 _____
Jeremiah 1:5 _____
Jeremiah 29:11 _____
John 1:12 _____
John 8:36 _____

John 10:4 _____

Galatians 3:29 _____

Colossians 2:10 _____

Romans 5:1 _____

Romans 8:37 _____

Philippians 4:13 _____

Ephesians 1:3 _____

Ephesians 2:10 _____

Hebrews 13:21 _____

2 Corinthians 2:15 _____

2 Corinthians 5:20 _____

1 Peter 2:9 _____

1 John 4:10 _____

Circle the top 3-5 attributes from above that really speak to your heart.

In medieval times, a shield with its coat of arms was a sign of identity and family lineage. In Ephesians 6, Paul describes the shield as part of our armor:

"In all circumstances take up the shield of faith, with which you can extinguish all the flaming darts of the evil one." Ephesians 6:16 ESV

Now write the 3-5 attributes you circled on the shield. Write the name God calls you on the banner.

This "shield of faith" is part of your protection against the enemy. Your name together with these attributes form your identity which is your shield of faith against the lies that the enemy hurls against your identity.

Choose to come into agreement with who God says you are.

Go Forward: Embrace Your Identity
To put this into practice, I want you to "wear" your new identity. Just like you'd try on a new outfit and see what you think in the mirror, I'd like for you to look in the mirror and speak out loud your identity in Christ by claiming each attribute. For example, if you wrote the attribute "chosen" on your shield. I want you to say, "I am chosen." Continue doing this every day until you believe it!

I also want you to use your God-given imagination and envision yourself as God sees you based on what you placed on your shield. How does a person with these attributes feel? What do they think? How do they act? How do they talk? Write out the answers in your journal for each attribute.

Example:

1 Peter 2:9 I am chosen

Someone chosen is not jealous of anyone else or their giftings, stands confident in who they are, they feel like they are able to do whatever asked, feel like they are enough, feel special.

How does it feel to talk to the Lord about the identity He's given you? Does He have more to add? Talk to God and journal your thoughts and prayers on the next page.

Continue
We've cleansed and cultivated, now we consider how we can continue walking this out.

Above all else, guard your heart, for everything you do flows from it.
Proverbs 4:23 NIV

Finally, brothers and sisters, whatever is true, whatever is noble, whatever is right, whatever is pure, whatever is lovely, whatever is admirable—if anything is excellent or praiseworthy—think about such things. Philippians 4:8 NIV

If we are allowing trash, the opposite of Philippians 4:8, to enter our hearts and minds, it won't be long before the lies are back! So, to continue, we need to watch over and guard what we let enter our hearts and minds. We need to ask the Lord to help us become aware of where we may be letting our shields down. Then we need to set some boundaries around those activities, thoughts, or people.

We can also go back to all we've journaled and written down in our missions about who God says we are and put truth journaling into regular practice.

Go Forward: Interact with the Word
The world's view of boundaries is often negative and restrictive. What does God say? Meditate on Psalm 16, inspecting a few different translations and reflecting on what God says about boundaries.

Record and pile up your "Memorial stones" from Mission #6 now:

MISSION SEVEN
Experience Freedom

At this point in your journey, you may be feeling pretty satisfied and ready to start working on your physical body. But we have potential roadblocks that we need to address before we can move on. I've seen unhealed heart wounds lead to using food, alcohol, or exercise to handle these wounds. Before we move on to the physical body, we have more internal work to do. I want you to walk in vibrant health with joy and peace, and so we need to consider what might be keeping us from this. I believe the root cause is not living in the present moment.

"Living in the present moment" was a new concept to me when I read the book, "Body, Mind & Health" by Monte Kline. [9] Kline reminds us that you can only live in three possible "moments"—the past, the future, and the present moment.

> "Despite protestations to the contrary, I find very few people who consistently live in the present moment. Most are imprisoned in either their past failures or their anticipated future glories. Either one represents considerable bondage."

"Imprisoned" is a powerful word! But thankfully, Jesus came to set captives free!

"The Spirit of the Lord is upon me, because he has anointed me to proclaim good news to the poor. He has sent me to proclaim liberty to the captives and recovering of sight to the blind, to set at liberty those who are oppressed, Luke 4:18 ESV

While there is benefit from looking back or looking ahead, it's when we get stuck there, "imprisoned," that causes us problems. The hurts and emotions from the past or fear of the future can keep us stuck and missing what God has for us in the now. I agreed with this new thought but was a bit shocked as well. Shocked that I was allowing misfocus to steal my peace and joy.

Let's examine another powerful quote, by Art Mathias of Wellspring Ministries:
"Fear and bitterness are two of the biggest blocks to healing."

The older I get the more truth I see in this statement by Mathias. The Lord connected the dots for me by combining Kline's thoughts with those of Mathias:
Imprisoned to the past will keep you stuck in bitterness and if chained to the future, you'll have constant fear and anxiety. There's no joy or health in these places!

God desires us to walk in freedom:

For freedom Christ has set us free; stand firm therefore, and do not submit again to a yoke of slavery. Galatians 5:1 ESV

Notice the end of the verse, "do not submit again to a yoke of slavery." How do we willingly tie ourselves to slavery? Look at these verses:

Be angry and do not sin; do not let the sun go down on your anger, and give no opportunity to the devil. Ephesians 4:26-27 ESV

But without faith it is impossible to please Him, for he who comes to God must believe that He is, and that He is a rewarder of those who diligently seek Him. Hebrews 11:6 NKJV

And whenever you stand praying, forgive, if you have anything against anyone, so that your Father also who is in heaven may forgive you your trespasses. Mark 11:25 ESV

"Therefore do not be anxious about tomorrow, for tomorrow will be anxious for itself. Sufficient for the day is its own trouble. Matthew 6:34 ESV

Why, you do not even know what will happen tomorrow. What is your life? You are a mist that appears for a little while and then vanishes. James 4:14 NIV

For God has not given us a spirit of fear, but of power and of love and of a sound mind. 2 Timothy 1:7 NKJV

Let all bitterness and wrath and anger and clamor and slander be put away from you, along with all malice. Ephesians 4:31 ESV

This is just a small sampling, but from it, we can see some things that could be hindering our freedom and joy: anger, bitterness, doubt, anxiety, fear, and unforgiveness. These are the strongholds, arguments and opinions that can keep us sick and stuck, lacking joy. This battle is not in the flesh...

For though we walk in the flesh, we are not waging war according to the flesh. For the weapons of our warfare are not of the flesh but have divine power to destroy strongholds. We destroy arguments and every lofty opinion raised against the knowledge of God, and take every thought captive to obey Christ, being ready to punish every disobedience, when your obedience is complete. 2 Corinthians 10:3-6 ESV

We are going to unpack and work through the two big hindrances to finding joy in the present, bitterness and fear. Let's allow God to renew our minds and heal our hearts so we can experience joy and peace.

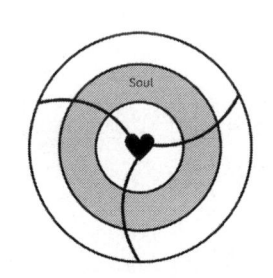

We want to keep in mind our 3C process and work on cleansing first which looks like forgiveness here. Then go to the Lord and His Word to cultivate and renew your mind. Then finish with continue as you yield and surrender to Him.

To cleanse, we have to stop and identify our strongholds and the arguments and opinions we are facing. You will need to ask the Lord to show you who and what you need to confess and release. This is not necessarily a fun process but it's vital to walking in freedom and joy!

You will need to get some paper—I prefer paper that can be thrown away. As you read through the next few pages you want to reflect by writing it out, hashing it out with God, and then moving on and throwing that paper full of hurts and lies away!

Check for Obstacle of Bitterness
Bitterness, resentfulness, and anger are all expressions of the root of unforgiveness.

See to it that no one fails to obtain the grace of God; that no "root of bitterness" springs up and causes trouble, and by it many become defiled; Hebrews 12:15 ESV

There are three objects of love – God, yourself, and others – and three obstacles to unforgiveness.

And you shall love the Lord your God with all your heart and with all your soul and with all your mind and with all your strength.' The second is this: 'You shall love your neighbor as yourself.' There is no other commandment greater than these.
Mark 12:30-31 ESV

Love Yourself - Forgive Yourself
We are to love others like we love ourselves, but many of us don't love ourselves. We are really hard on ourselves. You might be the hardest person you ever have to forgive. We talked about rejecting our identity in the last mission; and although it's similar, take this opportunity to see if you need to also forgive yourself.

I still have some tender spots in my heart from a time I personally had refused to forgive myself because I thought I deserved punishment. I had asked for God's forgiveness for a sin, but I couldn't seem to forgive myself. It took me a long time, too long, to be free of it! Jesus paid for it all at the cross! To hold onto unforgiveness is like saying that what Jesus did on the cross was not enough. It's time to let it go!

Go Forward
Are you holding onto something because you think you deserve punishment? What trash talk are you speaking to yourself? What are you not forgiving yourself for?

As you think about these things, ask Holy Spirit to reveal what needs to be forgiven:
- Sin of things done, or not done
- Condemning yourself
- "Should's"
- Religious spirit
- Valuing others' opinions more than God's; fear of man
- Lack of trust, carrying burdens we weren't meant to carry
- Unbelief

Example prayer:

Heavenly Father, I confess and repent of my sin of self-bitterness. I ask you to forgive me. I purpose and choose to forgive myself for this self-bitterness and/or self-hatred. In the name of Jesus, I cancel Satan's authority over me because I believed his lies. Holy Spirit, I invite you to heal me of self-bitterness. Please speak your words of truth to me about this situation.

Throw away the trash paper—those lies you were believing. Write in your journal the truth the Lord revealed that you want to remember.

Go back to your identity from mission #6, and your shield of identity. Go back to the mirror and speak over yourself who God says you are and receive the Father's love—let it wash over you.

Loving Others - Forgiving Others

Now consider people who have wronged you. Holding onto these wrongs is like holding on to trash. If you kept bags of trash in your living room all week while waiting for trash day, it would stink. If all you did was spray some air freshener, it would still stink. And it would be an ongoing thing you'd deal with over and over again every day. BUT if you take that trash out, that stink would be eliminated. You could sit in that room and enjoy. The same thing is happening with your body. You are holding on to trash - and not just for a week, but for years! It stinks!!! Are you ready to stop looking at and smelling that trash?

Go Forward

Grab another sheet of that throw-away paper and make a list of names as the Spirit brings them to mind. Right now, list those bags of trash. Name them and then forgive and release them. You are not doing it because they deserve it. You are not letting them off the hook for what they did—you are handing them on that hook over to God. He will deal with them. Forgiveness can't be based on your feelings. This is a choice you need to make because Jesus asked you to.

And whenever you stand praying, forgive, if you have anything against anyone, so that your Father also who is in heaven may forgive you your trespasses.
Mark 11:25 ESV

Bearing with one another and, if one has a complaint against another, forgiving each other; as the Lord has forgiven you, so you also must forgive.
Colossians 3:13 ESV

Pray a prayer of forgiveness over every name on your list.

Example prayer:
I purpose and choose to forgive _____ for _____
I release them and cancel their debt to me.
In the name of Jesus, I cancel all Satan's authority over me in this memory, because it is forgiven. Holy Spirit, heal my heart of all bitterness and show me God's truth about this situation. I declare my trust in You, God—the Righteous Judge. In Jesus name, Amen.

Love God - Forgive God
God doesn't sin, and yet we sometimes hold him hostage to wrongs we perceive He's done or allowed.

In Psalm 13:1-2 (NLT) David wrestled with this:
O LORD, how long will you forget me? Forever?
How long will you look the other way?
How long must I struggle with anguish in my soul, with sorrow in my heart every day? How long will my enemy have the upper hand?

Are you looking at current circumstances that are not great? Stuck remembering good things in your past? Or stuck holding Him to blame for all the bad that happened?

Has it made you angry and bitter at God? Any grudge that you may be holding against God is affecting your relationship. It's keeping you from loving God and more importantly, receiving His love because of the wall it's created. Although we aren't actually forgiving God, because He can't sin, you may need to go through steps similar to forgiveness. God is a good Father who will work things for your good.

I consider that our present sufferings are not worth comparing with the glory that will be revealed in us. Romans 8:18 NIV

And we know that in all things God works for the good of those who love him, who have been called according to his purpose. Romans 8:28 NIV

Go Forward
If holding a grudge against God is a roadblock that you need to work through, stop here and spend time in the book of Job. Job experienced such great loss, and his feelings are raw and real with God. There's a reason it is included in the Bible. It's not a quick read, so if you need to find a focus point reflect on Job 38:1-42:6.

I don't have an example prayer here, but I believe you'll have the conversations with God that are needed if you spend time in Job. Finally, you may need to surrender or repent of the grudge and the wall it created so the connection to His heart can be restored. I pray you'll give Him the space to do so!

I pray that this section was helpful and helped you begin the healing process. This is a continual process, and now that you know what kind of effect unforgiveness can have, I hope you'll be quick to come back and deal with it.

Now let's look at the roadblock of being stuck in a negative future-focused mindset.

Check for Obstacle of Fear
Fear fills us with an urgency to fix things and gives us a false sense of control. I see quite a few ladies, me included, getting sidetracked by this. I think motherhood sets us up for this trap—we get bogged down in all the things we do for our kids. When we get some mastery over it, then we become the "Master Fixers" that I warned about at the beginning of the book. Master Fixers try to do it all and stop trusting in the Lord.

At some point, you come to the end of yourself, broken and crying out to God. That's what happened to me. I controlled and planned and fixed all that I could, all while making sure we looked good to outsiders. But that's a lot to carry, and my mental health began to take a hit. I found myself anxious and trying out some supplements to alleviate the problem. Still not fully trusting in the Lord until the day came that I felt a panic attack coming, the day that marked a change in me.

This is the verse I clung to, the promise I claimed!

"For I am the LORD your God who takes hold of your right hand, Who says to you, 'Do not fear, I will help you.' Isaiah 41:13 NASB

That day that marked a complete change of course, I didn't even know what a panic attack was. I just felt like I could scream, run, cry or maybe just explode all at the same time and I did not feel like myself. I fled my house and drove down the street and sat outside on the grass and had a heart-to-heart with God. I gave it over. I let Him know I was done trying to fix things, and I needed Him to show up. Oh, how I wish I had gotten there sooner. I think

He is such a gentleman. He was graciously waiting for me to ask Him for help. Why oh why would I wait so long to ask? I spent quite a while in tears before I literally asked God, "Now what?" and the song, "I Surrender All" instantly played in my head. I actually laughed out loud at that moment. It was so practical and just the answer I needed. It's in these small things that I realize just how much He loves me!

I sought the LORD, and he answered me; he delivered me from all my fears. Psalm 34:4 NIV

Go Forward - Interact with the Word
How do you counter fear and anxiety? What is the truth we need to come back into alignment with?

Let God's Word and His promises bridge the gap between the fear you feel and what you know to be true about God and His love for you. Record what these Scriptures say. Spend time cleansing any lies you've been believing and ask God for the promises from His Word to renew your mind. (cleanse & cultivate)

Psalm 37:5 _____
Hebrews 13:5b-6 _____
Psalm 34:4 _____
2 Timothy 1:7 _____
Deuteronomy 31:6 _____
Jeremiah 17:7 _____
Psalm 46:1-3 _____
1 Peter 5:7 _____
Psalm 5:11 _____
Ephesians 4:7 _____

Our third C, Continue, is an act of yielding and surrendering. That is what's needed if you really want to live a life of joy.

We have to surrender that He alone is God.

Go Forward

How do we walk free of fear? It's in the song God gave me, surrender all. Control is an illusion of the enemy. Stop now and surrender all the outcomes and expectations you have. That's the simple, but not easy, action step that needs to happen here.

...offer yourselves to God as those who have been brought from death to life; and offer every part of yourself to him as an instrument of righteousness.
Romans 6:13b NIV

Let's move forward and capture the present moment...

You will show me the path of life; In Your presence is fullness of joy; At Your right hand are pleasures forevermore. Psalm 16:11 NKJV

Where does it say joy is? In His presence!

When we get stuck worrying about the future or chained to the past hurts or the wonderful times, we miss God in the present moment, and it leaves us lacking joy. It also steals our contentment and gratitude.

Do you love vacations? I think this is a prime example of living in the present moment. We go sit at the beach or somewhere fun and enjoy the people and the experiences around us. During a vacation, we often lay aside our past and future focuses, and we are intentional about enjoying the present. What would life look like if we were doing this in every moment, not just on vacation?

Practical Help
In Kline's book, he uses the phrase "capture the present moment." I love how he used "capture" since it requires intentional effort. We must choose to seek the present moment and God who is there with you in that moment. I believe your joy will be restored as you do this—no matter if your circumstances change or not.

How do you capture the present moment?

Here are some ideas that you might consider:
- Stop multitasking, focus on one thing, and give it your focus.
- Slow down. Consider practicing a breath prayer to help you refocus (example was given in Mission #5).
- Use all your senses to take in the present moment: the sights, smells, conversations, feelings, and tastes. Literally name 5 things you see, 4 things you hear, 3 things you can feel, 2 things you smell, and one thing you taste.
- As you do all the above, look for the good, feel the emotions (laugh, smile, cry) and worship and thank God for it all.

Record and pile up your "Memorial stones" from Mission #7 now:

NOTE: There are deep issues that may come up in this mission. If trauma, abuse, or occult practices are part of your past, you may benefit more by walking through this mission with a Christian counselor. I don't pretend to be one! I've just listed the methods and prayers that have been helpful for me.

MISSION EIGHT
Fit and fueled to run with purpose

This mission is not about actual physical running—although you can if you want. This mission is about our vision of living in vibrant health, so we are able to run with purpose the race God has for us.

IF you skipped ahead to this mission just waiting for me to tell you what you can and can't eat.... you missed it! Go back. Everything BEFORE this mission is more important. Why? Because no diet, no exercise plan, and no supplement exists to fix the things that affect your spirit and soul and those two areas of you—fuel your life, your attitude, your vision, and your purpose!

In 1 Corinthians 9, Paul gives us instruction for how to run, look for how he describes it:

Do you not know that in a race all the runners run, but only one receives the prize? So run that you may obtain it. Every athlete exercises self-control in all things. They do it to receive a perishable wreath, but we an imperishable. So I do not run aimlessly; I do not box as one beating the air. But I discipline my body and keep it under control, lest after preaching to others I myself should be disqualified. 1 Corinthians 9:24-27 ESV

Did you highlight these descriptions for how to run?
"Run that you may obtain it"
"Do not run aimlessly"
"I discipline my body and keep it under control."

Entire books have been written on how to care for the body. In fact, we have been flooded with information. I'm guessing you have some pretty solid ideas on how to care for your physical body already. We are going to keep a high-level Biblical view from 1 Corinthians 9 in mind as we travel through this mission. For our purpose we want to examine how we can steward this body, discipline it, so it's able to run with purpose.

Let's look at two verses from God's Word, the Truth that will serve as an anchor:

So God created man in his own image, in the image of God he created him; male and female he created them. Genesis 1:27 ESV

Or do you not know that your body is a temple of the Holy Spirit within you, whom you have from God? You are not your own, for you were bought with a price. So glorify God in your body. 1 Corinthians 6:19-20 ESV

Your body was made in the image of God, it was purchased with Christ's blood and now it is the dwelling place of His Spirit. It is beautiful, it is special and it is important to God!

Keep these truths as your focus as we use the 3C's to help us walk through the process. The purpose here is simple and foundational. I'm giving you the high-level foundations everyone will want to start with before going deeper, if needed.

Notice we are not talking about a number on a bathroom scale in this mission. We can all live with purpose at different sizes. So, this mission has nothing to do with your weight. Choose to love yourself just as you are! Choose to love yourself if you never lose a pound, never fix those teeth, or never get rid of the gray hair because your Father loves you the way you are right now. This is why we spent time on identity in mission 6.

Your body is your God-created vehicle specifically made for you and your call! You need it to go forward with purpose. Let's get started with cleansing...

Cleanse

Cleansing can look like:
- Avoiding or limiting low octane food
- Avoiding toxic products
- Drinking plenty of clean water
- Occasional fasting

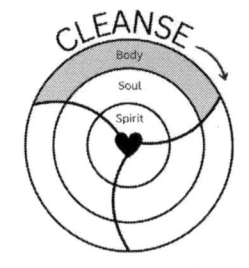

Don't be misled—you cannot mock the justice of God. You will always harvest what you plant. Galatians 6:7 NLT

Galatians 6 tells us about the principle of sowing and reaping. It's the principle that tells us we can't expect to have a tomato if we planted a potato.

What have you sown in your body to get your current harvest? It will take some time of reflection and honesty with yourself to discover. The intent here is not shame or condemnation but just an honest assessment of those things that are not helping you run your race.

What harvest do you want?
What needs to be cleansed and planted to reap that harvest?
Step one is cleansing the things that are reaping unwanted results.

Go Forward - Assess your current harvest
Assess your current harvest. Maybe you've been running full steam ahead—and you don't even know what's going on. Find some time to stop, breathe and really see how your body feels. Record the date and how you are feeling using the questions below to help you assess. Let this assessment be an indicator of opportunities to steward the body better. Let it show you some of the things that need to be cleansed.

What are you feeling?
Are you in pain or can you move freely without pain?
Where are you holding tension?
How are you sleeping?
What is your energy like? Do you have the energy to do the things you'd like to do?
Also consider how food has affected your body recently.
What slows your body down? What causes inflammation and/or pain? What makes your brain feel fuzzy? What makes you feel like taking a nap? What keeps you awake? What makes you feel grouchy or on edge?

Date:

Food is Fuel

Let's talk about food as fuel for our physical body. When we think of food as fuel, consider low octane and premium high-octane fuel for your vehicle. The higher the octane, the cleaner and better the return you get in how your vehicle runs. The same is true with food for your body.

High octane fuel for our bodies will be closer to how God created it. It will have less ingredients, preservatives, and chemicals. Think of fresh fruits and vegetables, eggs, etc. in this category.

Low octane fuel is more processed and sometimes even completely manufactured chemical foods. Foods that fit here would be most things that come packaged in plastic and boxes with a long list of ingredients, especially sugary foods.

Many of you have experienced food causing a negative effect, perhaps with wheat or dairy. For others who've never been taught to observe the body for signals of stress, we just don't know. That's ok! Just know that food can and does affect your energy levels, your mood, sleep and so many other things that can determine how your body runs. It might look like sleepiness right after you eat, or bloating or a fuzzy brain. For others, crazy emotions, or no sleep. Be on the lookout for any signs of how food is affecting you.

I'm not giving you a DO and DO NOT eat list. Every person is unique, and each has different foods that fuel them best. At each meal you have options, and I'd love for you to make better quality choices. Some days we are blessed with fresh produce and meats, other days we are choosing the best of the low octane…that's just reality! Working, traveling, finances, and many other factors affect our choices.

The goal here is awareness of what fuels your body best and limiting or removing the things that are poor fuel for you. I encourage you to make your own list of foods. What is low octane for you? What is high octane? What falls in the middle?

Low Octane   **High Octane**

Assist Cleansing

Cleansing can look like avoiding low octane foods and adding in things that assist the body in cleansing. Because even good things, if stuck in the body, can become toxic, so we want to always promote cleansing.

Since we have these promises, beloved, let us cleanse ourselves from every defilement of body and spirit, bringing holiness to completion in the fear of God. 2 Corinthians 7:1 ESV

Water is a must! Our body cannot properly operate and cleanse itself without adequate clean water. We need to find a way to incorporate it in our daily habits. You'll often hear that you need to drink half your weight in ounces of water each day. When I first started with this goal, I wore a few stretchy bracelets around my wrist to remind me. Each one represented one full water bottle and I would move one to my other wrist each time I finished a bottle. The goal was to move all my bracelets to the opposite wrist by the end of the day. Find something that works for you! At the end of this chapter, I have a tracker that you may find helpful as well.

Fasting is a wonderful spiritual practice but also a beneficial one for the physical body as well. This can give the body a break from digesting food so that it can clean. It can be a huge help to getting our body back on track physically. I've experienced restoration in body, soul, and spirit from my times of fasting. Many years ago, I had issues that didn't resolve after getting off birth control. I finally went on a fast that helped cleanse the body and it was very effective in helping me get back to normal.

We also need to consider non-food items that affect the body: usually these come in the form of toxic chemicals we breathe in or slather on our bodies. The skin is your biggest organ. Conventional Doctors use patches to deliver prescription medicines. Why on the skin? Because these drugs are absorbed straight into the bloodstream from the skin bypassing the liver. A similar thing happens when you slather toxic products on your skin. Candles, fragrances, lotions, makeup, cleaning products and so many things like that are loaded with unhealthy chemicals that can affect our hormones, gut health and more. I do believe when my family made the switch to toxin-free products over ten years ago that this made a huge impact on our health. I realized we were getting sick a lot less frequently!

Cultivate
Cultivate is the process of adding in things that will help produce growth.

Other seeds fell on good soil and produced grain, some a hundredfold, some sixty, some thirty. He who has ears, let him hear. Matthew 13:8-9 ESV

Cultivating the land produces good soil – good soil that God can use and multiply your harvest. As you examine the following items, consider how they will help produce a greater harvest.

Cultivating can look like:
- Eating high octane fuel in a mindful way
- Intentionally moving the body
- Regular times to be still with the Lord
- Getting restorative sleep

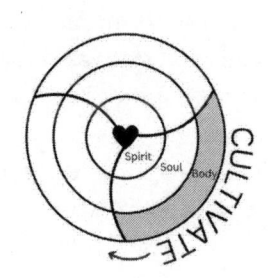

High Octane Fuel
High octane fuel is important. The more high-octane foods we can incorporate, the better our body will run. Because many of us have been neglecting the body for quite some time, supplementation may be beneficial to getting us back on track faster. But start with food—you have to eat anyway—so that's the place to start.

Mindful Eating
Mindful eating is a "living in the present moment" practice that has physical and spiritual benefits. What fuel we give the body matters but also how we consume food affects how the body runs. As a naturopath, the first thing we correct are digestive problems because they influence everything else in the body.

Dr. Emeran Mayer says, "the gut can influence our basic emotions, our pain sensitivity, and our social interactions, and even guide many of our decisions—and not just those about our food preferences and meal sizes." [10]

Mindful eating can often improve digestive problems and how the body runs on the fuel we give it.
Here are the practical suggestions I offer my clients:
- Breathe, slow down, smell your food which will help switch the body into parasympathetic mode and better prepare it to digest and absorb the fuel.
- Engage the senses to experience the food and be thankful for it.
- Chew food well to ensure food is properly broken down, as well as to be enjoyed.
- Limit liquids with meals, so you don't dilute the stomach acid and prevent proper digestion.

LIVE IN VIBRANT HEALTH

- Know what physical hunger feels like, often a burning in the stomach and slight physical weakness.
- Consume food when the body is actually hungry, not because of hard-to-handle emotions or boredom.
- Learn and notice the signs of being satisfied and stop eating before you are stuffed.
- Notice the effects food has on your body and mood.

Check for Obstacle
Our bodies were made to hunger. But not just physical hunger, we hunger for love, acceptance, and so much more. God made us this way....so we'd be hungry for HIM! But we often get things all mixed up and try to use physical food to feed an emotional hunger. This is the opposite of mindful eating; we call it emotional eating.

We emotionally eat to avoid our feelings and avoid confrontation with other people and God. We use it to avoid hard and messy things.

How can you address this?
You can pause before you eat, breathe, and assess – Do I have signs of physical hunger? What emotions am I feeling right now?

You can use a hunger scale to help you assess if you are physically hungry. (At the end of the mission there is a tracking page you can use as a tool if you'd like.)

Hunger Scale
1. Starving
2. Hungry
3. Satisfied
4. Full
5. Stuffed

If you are not physically hungry, then grab a journal to process your emotions and start the practice of truth journaling you learned in Mission #6.

Work

Then the LORD God took the man and put him in the Garden of Eden to cultivate it and tend it. Genesis 2:15 NASB

We were created to work, specifically from the beginning to cultivate the land. This job was given to Adam before he sinned, so it is not a punishment. God created us to move our bodies with physical labor.

Go Forward – Interact with the Word
Record what else is said in these verses:

Ecclesiastes 5:12 _____

Ephesians 4:28 _____

1 Thessalonians 4:11-12 _____

2 Thessalonians 3:10-12 _____

The Ancient Greeks, known for giving us the Olympics, glorified the body. Things got twisted then and are twisted now! Our bodies were made to worship, not be worshiped. The glorification of the body and the idol of exercise is seen everywhere we look. We don't want to fall into this trap. This is not about creating more rules, it's about opening a door to a better way. A door that can lead to peace, strength, health, and confidence.

Check for Obstacle
We can fall into a ditch on either side of the road during our journey. One ditch is neglecting the body. The other ditch is obsessing over the body. It's also easy to be so motivated to get out of one ditch that we end up catapulting ourselves into the other ditch!

So how do we flip the script?
If you are neglecting movement, how do you stop seeing it as punishment or drudgery?
If you've been obsessing over working out, how can you make movement about worship?

I think the answer is here:

Therefore, since we are surrounded by such a huge crowd of witnesses to the life of faith, let us strip off every weight that slows us down, especially the sin that so easily trips us up. And let us run with endurance the race God has set before us. We do this by keeping our eyes on Jesus, the champion who initiates and perfects our faith. Because of the joy awaiting him, he endured the cross, disregarding its shame. Now he is seated in the place of honor beside God's throne.
Hebrews 12:1-2 NLT

Change the way you talk to yourself about moving.

Declare it now... I get to move! I get to worship!

Sabbath

God instituted Sabbath because we need rest.

Six days you shall labor, and do all your work, but the seventh day is a Sabbath to the LORD your God. On it you shall not do any work - Exodus 20:9-10a ESV

Be still, and know that I am God. I will be exalted among the nations, I will be exalted in the earth! Psalm 46:10 ESV

We talked about being still in Mission #5, but I wanted to bring it up again because it does help the physical body. Breathing and being still can activate our parasympathetic nervous system which controls the rest and repair of the body. This can influence digestion and your hormones in a big way too.

But we don't just need times of stillness, we need restorative sleep. You can find studies on the benefits of sleep for physical and mental health everywhere. Here's a sampling of quotes from just one resource.

Matthew Walker's "Why We Sleep: Unlocking the Power of Sleep and Dreams"

> "...the shorter your sleep, the shorter your life. The leading causes of disease and death in developed nations—diseases that are crippling health-care systems, such as heart disease, obesity, dementia, diabetes, and cancer—all have recognized causal links to a lack of sleep."

> "Routinely sleeping less than six or seven hours a night demolishes your immune system, more than doubling your risk of cancer."

> "When sleep is abundant, minds flourish. When it is deficient, they don't." [11]

I notice such a change in my mental health from just one night of lost sleep that I just don't like to feel that way. So, bedtime is a priority and oftentimes I give myself days to sleep in with no alarm.

What are you doing to encourage restorative sleep? Consider the time you need to restore and repair.

This quote by Walker may help you realize just how important this is:

> "After thirty years of intensive research, we can now answer many of the questions posed earlier. The recycle rate of a human being is around sixteen hours. After sixteen hours of being awake, the brain begins to fail. Humans need more than seven hours of sleep each night to maintain cognitive performance."

Continue

To continue means we need to stay committed to the vision of vibrant health—to steward the body so it's fit and fueled to run with purpose.
Read 1 Corinthians 9:24-27 again:

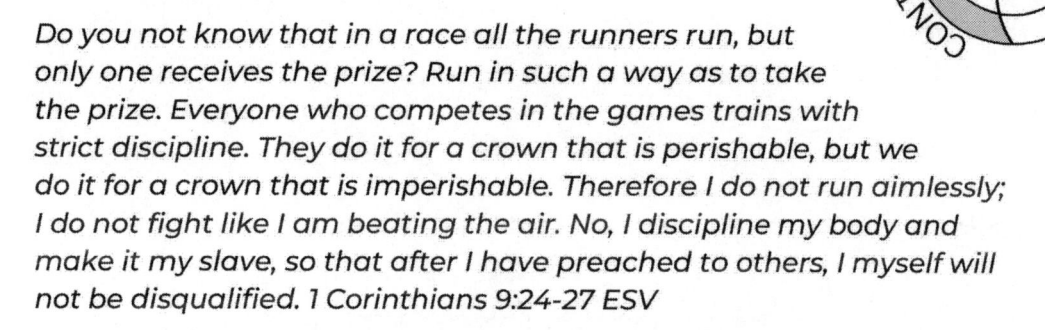

Do you not know that in a race all the runners run, but only one receives the prize? Run in such a way as to take the prize. Everyone who competes in the games trains with strict discipline. They do it for a crown that is perishable, but we do it for a crown that is imperishable. Therefore I do not run aimlessly; I do not fight like I am beating the air. No, I discipline my body and make it my slave, so that after I have preached to others, I myself will not be disqualified. 1 Corinthians 9:24-27 ESV

This means we have to keep focused on the finish line, so we aren't running aimlessly.

No discipline seems pleasant at the time, but painful. Later on, however, it produces a harvest of righteousness and peace for those who have been trained by it. Hebrews 12:11 NIV

Earlier I asked, "What do you want to harvest?" Consider that question again and journal your thoughts.

Something to look out for is taking control too far and letting it sabotage your journey where you land back in the ditch of obsession. We don't want to make a religion out of exercise or the perfect diet. Big sweeping changes all at once can lead to pride and changes that don't last. This can come and take over just like emotional eating can lead us down a negative path. We are doing something positive but, in a controlling, obsessive way to avoid dealing with hard things.

I successfully followed the keto diet for a time, lost weight and looked good. Looking back, I believe I was grasping for something to control because I couldn't control a lot of other things that were going on. I was avoiding hard and messy emotions.

Step 3, Continue, is the process of continuing our walk with the Lord, yielded and moldable. It's a delicate place to walk, but one that will bring much fruit.

Tools
Tracking forms or apps can be wonderful tools to stay focused and prevent you from running aimlessly. I've included a tracking sheet for you to observe those habits that will help you run towards the finish line as well as to observe and assess what you are harvesting. These tracking tools are an opportunity to help you make better choices. They can help you translate your good intentions into behavior that gets you to the finish line.

Be aware that tracking tools can also be tools of destruction if you become a slave to them. Use them for a time to help you learn new habits and be intentional, but also know that you don't need them when you let the Holy Spirit be your guide.

"May God himself, the God who makes everything holy and whole, make you holy and whole, put you together–spirit, soul and body–and keep you fit for the coming of our Master, Jesus Christ. The One who called you is completely dependable. If he said it, he'll do it." 1 Thessalonians 5:23-24 MSG

Record and pile up your "Memorial stones" from Mission #8 now:

Download a digital copy of the tracker at LiveinVibrantHealth.com

daily tracker

Water - each drop represents 10oz

◊ ◊ ◊ ◊ ◊ ◊ ◊ ◊ ◊

1-starving 2-hungry 3-satisfied 4-full 5-stuffed

○ **BREAKFAST**

○ **LUNCH**

○ **DINNER**

○ **SNACKS**

WEEKLY FOCUS

DATE: _____

♡ **CONNECT TO GOD**

TODAY'S TOP GOALS

#1.

#2.

#3.

○

SUPPLEMENTS   am   pm

MOVEMENT

○

Restorative Sleep ★★★★★   Energy & Mood ★★★★★

○

NOTES

_____
_____
_____
_____

LIVE IN VIBRANT HEALTH

MISSION NINE
Live to shine

We've come a long way in this journey!

Let's recap the journey so far. You have:
- Established a higher purpose for health
- Grasped the need to work inside out
- Practiced cleansing, cultivating, and continuing in all areas of life
- Connected to the Father's heart
- Come into agreement with who He says you are
- Let go of fear and bitterness
- Soaked up joy in His presence
- Learned how to fuel your body to run with purpose

These achievements have only been accomplished by the power of the Holy Spirit at work. Praise Him for the work of transformation that's taken place so far in your journey, making you into a vibrant woman.

We started off Mission #1 with your YES and we end our journey transformed and with the same question.... will you say YES to Him?

The Christian walk is a journey of YES's!
Now, will you say Yes to walking in vibrant health in a way that shines for His glory?

Let your light so shine before men, that they may see your good works and glorify your Father in heaven. Matthew 5:16 NKJV

Your YES will inspire someone else to say yes!
That's what "live to shine" means!

My YES brought me on the journey of writing a book, something I never aspired to do. Although I felt God called me to write, there were times of doubt, confusion, and conflicting thoughts along the way. I had to press in and seek God more and more and I had to keep saying yes.

Sometimes I felt unequipped, and I took some breaks. It was during a break that God gave me a dream one night—really more like two pictures. The first was a large black stick which I didn't recognize and asking God, "What is that?" He immediately answered, "a cattle prod." The second picture was a sheathed cattle prod being handed to me. The next day I got up and googled "cattle prod" because I really didn't know what that was. I learned it is used to give an electric shock to cattle to get them moving. From the first picture, I felt like God was prompting me to get going; my book needed to be finished!

The second picture I believe was Him telling me that I'm supposed to hand a cattle prod to others. I'm to challenge or prod you as a vibrant woman to say yes to more—to go and "live to shine" just as the Lord prodded me to do.

Did you ever sing this as a child?

> *This little light of mine, I'm gonna let it shine!*
> *This little light of mine, I'm gonna let it shine!*
> *Let it shine, let it shine, let it shine*
> *Hide it under a bushel? No, I'm gonna let it shine.*
> *Won't let Satan (blow) it out, I'm gonna let it shine.*
> *Let it shine till Jesus comes, I'm gonna let it shine.*

Simple truths we teach children but forget as we age. We lose our child-like faith. I know I have forgotten many times. I've disqualified myself. I've hid my light. I've let circumstances and the enemy blow out my light. What about you?

Check for Obstacle
I want to stop before going further because there's a big trap we want to avoid. You may have fallen for it before, and I don't want you to get stuck in this again.

There is a difference between DOing and BEing.

The world's way is DO first and what you've accomplished defines your purpose and your identity. But with God, it's different. First, we BE and have our purpose in Christ – and then we go and DO out of this identity.

DOing first will leave us stuck in striving and lost purpose and identity. There is no joy in this! And it leaves us stuck in religion and legalism.

Go Forward: Cleanse & Cultivate
You are enough because Christ in you is enough! You are called to shine!
I'd like for the Word to cleanse any of your false ideas and renew your mind about who you should BE in Christ.

We tend to read the same Bible version over and over and often get stuck in understanding it the same way. For this reason, I've included particular versions here for a new perspective. You may want to go ahead and write them out or just read them slowly. Ask the Holy Spirit to highlight words or phrases for you to focus on.

We have become his poetry, a re-created people that will fulfill the destiny he has given each of us, for we are joined to Jesus, the Anointed One. Even before we were born, God planned in advance our destiny and the good works we would do to fulfill it! Ephesians 2:10 TPT

For you were once darkness, but now you are light in the Lord. Live as children of light. Ephesians 5:8 NIV

For it is the God who commanded light to shine out of darkness, who has shone in our hearts to give the light of the knowledge of the glory of God in the face of Jesus Christ. 2 Corinthians 4:6 NKJV

So, my dear brothers and sisters, be strong and immovable. Always work enthusiastically for the Lord, for you know that nothing you do for the Lord is ever useless. 1 Corinthians 15:58 NLT

It's in Christ that we find out who we are and what we are living for. Long before we first heard of Christ and got our hopes up, he had his eye on us, had designs on us for glorious living, part of the overall purpose he is working out in everything and everyone. Ephesians 1:11-12 MSG

Instead fully immerse yourselves into the Lord Jesus, the Anointed One, and don't waste even a moment's thought on your former identity to awaken its selfish desires. Romans 13:14 TPT

Who should you BE in Christ?

Continue
The phrase "live to shine" is what I felt God called me to do. But really, it's not about doing it's more about BEING. It's about choosing to wake up each day and being who God designed me to be.

Go Forward
Contemplate Colossians 3

And whatever you do, whether in word or deed, do it all in the name of the Lord Jesus, giving thanks to God the Father through him. Colossians 3:17 NIV

Maybe he said "whatever you do" because the doing part doesn't matter as much as the character of being he lists in the previous verses 12-16

Therefore, as God's chosen people, holy and dearly loved, clothe yourselves with compassion, kindness, humility, gentleness and patience. Bear with each other and forgive one another if any of you has a grievance against someone. Forgive as the Lord forgave you. And over all these virtues put on love, which binds them all together in perfect unity. Let the peace of Christ rule in your hearts, since as members of one body you were called to peace. And be thankful. Let the message of Christ dwell among you richly as you teach and admonish one another with all wisdom through psalms, hymns, and songs from the Spirit, singing to God with gratitude in your hearts. Colossians 3:12-16 NIV

What does "live to shine" mean for you?
You are going to write out what "live to shine" means to you through a personal manifesto.

> Manifesto = A public declaration, usually of a prince or sovereign, showing his intentions, or proclaiming his opinions and motives; as a manifesto declaring the purpose of a prince to begin war, and explaining his motives.

For your manifesto, I want you to think big and declare who you are to the world. You will declare what you believe at your core and why you exist. It will tell who you are and how you'll behave.

While a vision and mission statement are wonderful, they are often about what you will do and the outcomes you hope to achieve. Your manifesto is about "being" over "doing." Often God changes our course and the outcomes we sought never materialize. With the manifesto, we are yielding and surrendering to the outcome that the Lord wants. We'll declare that we will be who God made us and use it as a compass to keep us on track on our journey.

The Memorial Stones, those truths you wrote at the end of each mission, will be helpful here. Look back at those stones as you sit with the Lord and write your manifesto.

These questions may give you more to reflect on as well:
What makes me different?
What ways has God gifted me?
What do I value in others?
Who does God want me to be?
What motivates me?
What sparks His light in me?
What am I good at?
When do I feel most satisfied in Him?
What does God want me to speak into others?

How will you live this out? Who will you be? Write some declarations...
  Examples:
    I embody joy
    I have purpose
    I bring peace wherever I go
    I am bold with the truth

Clearly and concisely make your statements beginning with the word "I."
Use positive wording. Avoid the words "will" or "try" - we are making bold declarations.

Now we are going to refine it. I am giving you a beginning and ending statement, personalize and fill in the middle section from your declarations on the previous page.

I am a Vibrant Woman

_____

_____

_____

_____

_____

_____

I live to shine

This is not to be done alone! Press in and listen to your Father. He created you uniquely with great purpose. Listen in and hear what He has to say!

This doesn't have to be perfect, write what comes to mind and let God rework it over time if needed. As you grow and seek God, it may evolve and that's beautiful.

Go Forward
I'd like you to make your declarations known!

I want you to read your completed manifesto out loud to yourself for the next seven days. How does it feel? Do you feel aligned with God? Adjust as needed and as God grows and continues the transformation process in you.

Then go share online #ilivetoshine #shinemanifesto and send it to me. I'd love to read your Manifesto!

"Your purpose is not the thing you do. It is the thing that happens in others when you do what you do." ~ Dr. Caroline Leaf

And let us consider how we may spur one another on toward love and good deeds, Hebrews 10:24 NIV

When you shine, confident in your identity in Christ, you won't see anyone else as competition. No, we are all teammates. Individually we each have burdens for the lost in different ways. But together, on Team Jesus, we are burdened for everyone. When we each shine, we can reach the world together with the gospel of Christ!

Go and live to shine Vibrant Woman!

Vibrant Health Framework™

CLEANSE

Body

Soul

Spirit

CULTIVATE

CONTINUE

APPENDIX
Why Jesus?

How did I find and get to know Jesus?

As a teenager, I was independent and a know-it-all master fixer. I had my life planned out, but things didn't go as planned. God showed me my need for Him through normal teenage disappointments.

I knew of Jesus; I had prayed a prayer – but I didn't have relationship with Him. The idea that I'm in control and then realizing when things start to fall like a house of cards that I really need Jesus – was a pattern I repeated a few times in life! At the age of 16 is the first time this happened and when Jesus became real to me. That night in my room, I surrendered it all – not unlike what happened to me later in life which you've read about in this book.

I wish I could say that I grew and figured all of this out quickly after my conversion at 16, but it didn't quite work out like that. I coasted for a lot of years until I couldn't anymore. The hardships and circumstances of life became deeper hurts to my heart and a hunger for real relationship with Jesus began. The journey that sent me searching for wellness was really a search for more of Him.

And that's what He's waiting for from you – for you to long for Him like He longs for you. He loved you before you were born! Jesus died for you out of His great love for you.

But God demonstrates his own love for us in this: While we were still sinners, Christ died for us. Romans 5:8 NIV

And He did it all, while knowing what you would do and how you would fail him.... but He did it anyway...and He invites you now into an authentic relationship with Him. No games, no need to clean up before you do anything.

But when the kindness and love of God our Savior appeared, he saved us, not because of righteous things we had done, but because of his mercy. He saved us through the washing of rebirth and renewal by the Holy Spirit, whom he poured out on us generously through Jesus Christ our Savior, so that, having been justified by his grace, we might become heirs having the hope of eternal life. Titus 3:4-7 NIV

Just cry out to Him!

If you declare with your mouth, "Jesus is Lord," and believe in your heart that God raised him from the dead, you will be saved. For it is with your heart that you believe and are justified, and it is with your mouth that you profess your faith and are saved. Romans 10:9-10 NIV

who God says I am

Chosen
JOHN 15:16

Gifted
ROMANS 11:29

Strong
PHILIPPIANS 4:13

Beloved
JEREMIAH 31:3

Known
JOHN 10:4

Complete
COLOSSIANS 2:10

Courageous
DEUTERONOMY 31:6

Sweet Aroma
2 CORINTHIANS 2:15

His Child
JOHN 1:12

Loved
1 JOHN 4:10

Victorious
ROMANS 8:37

Redeemed
ROMANS 3:24

Appointed
JEREMIAH 1:5

Equipped
HEBREWS 13:21

Masterpiece
EPHESIANS 2:10

Forgiven
EPHESIANS 1:7

Set apart
1 PETER 2:9-10

Wonderful
PSALM 139:13-17

Blessed
EPHESIANS 1:3

Precious
ISAIAH 43:4

Bold
2 CORINTHIANS 3:12

LIVE IN VIBRANT HEALTH

references

1. Connolly, Jess. *You Are the Girl for the Job: Daring to Believe the God Who Calls You.* Zondervan, 2019.

2. Rice Smith, Sherrie. *EFT for Christians.* Energy Psychology Press, 2015.

3. Virkler, Mark and Patti. *4 Keys to Hearing God's Voice.* Destiny Image Publishers, 2013.

4. Mathias, Art and Patti. *How to Minister Workbook.* Wellspring Ministries, 2008. Note: some of the example prayers throughout the book were adapted from this source

5. Barton, Ruth Haley. *Sacred Rhythms: Arranging Our Lives for Spiritual Transformation.* IVP, 2009.

6. Keeton, Alisa. *The Wellness Revelation: Lose What Weighs You Down so You Can Love God, Yourself, and Others.* Tyndale Momentum, 2017.

7. Millman, Dan. *Body Mind Mastery: Training For Sport and Life.* New World Library, 1999.

8. Raveling, Barb. *The Renewing of the Mind Project: Going to God for Help with Your Habits, Goals, and Emotions.* Truthway Press, 2015.

9. Kline, Monte. *Body, Mind & Health: Discovering God's Solutions for Total Health.* Independently published, 2014.

10. Mayer, Emeran. *The Mind-Gut Connection: How the Hidden Conversation Within Our Bodies Impacts Our Mood, Our Choices, and Our Overall Health.* Harper Wave, 2018.

11. Walker, Matthew. *Why We Sleep: Unlocking the Power of Sleep and Dreams.* Scribner, 2018.

Definitions from the 1828 Webster's Dictionary accessed from https://webstersdictionary1828.com/

about the author

Stephanie Tyler is a Traditional Naturopath offers holistic health coaching and fitness classes to help women walk in vibrant health in body, soul and spirit. Stephanie and her husband, Scott, make their home in Northwest Arkansas where she can often be found hosting a big family gathering, drinking coffee or reading a book.

Stephanie would love to hear how this study has impacted your life.

Send your manifesto and your stories to the author by visiting the website at:
LiveinVibrantHealth.com

This book forms the foundation of a mentorship that guides women through to realize their purpose and identity so they can find a higher purpose for pursuing vibrant health and truly shine!

For more information on the transformational program go to:
VibrantWomanReignited.com

If you are ready to develop yourself further and grow
to impact others in the Kingdom, go to:
ShinefortheKingdom.com